Like Ripples on Water

Like Ripples on Water

*On Russian Baptist Preaching, Identity,
and the Pulpit's Neglected Powers*

Timofey Cheprasov

Foreword by
Keith Grant Jones

WIPF & STOCK · Eugene, Oregon

LIKE RIPPLES ON WATER
On Russian Baptist Preaching, Identity, and the Pulpit's Neglected Powers

Copyright © 2018 Timofey Cheprasov. All rights reserved. Except for brief quotations in critical publications or reviews, no part of this book may be reproduced in any manner without prior written permission from the publisher. Write: Permissions, Wipf and Stock Publishers, 199 W. 8th Ave., Suite 3, Eugene, OR 97401.

Wipf & Stock
An Imprint of Wipf and Stock Publishers
199 W. 8th Ave., Suite 3
Eugene, OR 97401

www.wipfandstock.com

PAPERBACK ISBN: 978-1-5326-1766-9
HARDCOVER ISBN: 978-1-4982-4252-3
EBOOK ISBN: 978-1-4982-4251-6

Manufactured in the U.S.A.

"Preaching is the most important ministry of a spiritual laborer on God's field . . . Moving preaching to the background, he, therefore, lowers himself to a position of a human being who lost his true mission."

- N. N., ["Work on sermons"]. *BV* 5 (1969)

Contents

Foreword by Keith Grant Jones | xi
Acknowledgments | xv
Abbreviations | xvii
Translation and Transliteration | xviii
Preface | xxi

Chapter 1—Retelling the Story: The Beginning of the Russian Baptistic Movement | 1
    Introduction
    Russian Empire in the Second Half of the Nineteenth Century
        Freedom
        The Crisis
        The Bible
    The Stundist Dissent
    Conclusion

Chapter 2—Theological Nest of the Russian Orthodox Church | 13
    Introduction
    Theosis: The Way . . .
    . . . Walked Together with Others (Sobornost)
    Preaching in the Russian Orthodox Church
    Conclusion

Contents

Chapter 3—Development of Russian Baptist Preaching in the
Nineteenth and Twentieth Centuries | 25
    Introduction
    Formative Years
    Big Dreams and Dashed Hopes: 1905–1929
        The Christian Printed Media
        Christian Education
    Trials and Tribulations: Living in a Spiritual Desert, 1929–1987
        Atheistic Academia vs. Baptistic Spirituality
    Conclusion

Chapter 4—Preaching and *Bratskii Vestnik* | 51
    Introduction
    Biblical Exegesis in Post-war Publications
    Bratskii Vestnik on Preaching
    Conclusion

Chapter 5—Preaching in Contemporary Russian Baptist Churches | 65
    Introduction
    The Context of Worship
        Worship Pattern
        The *Ministers of the Word* and the Problem of Authority
    Contemporary Understanding of Preaching
    Conclusion

Chapter 6—The Need for a Vision: Defining Baptistic Identity | 78
    Introduction
    Various Ways to Define Baptist Identity
    A Story of the *Dobrovolets* [Volunteer] Community
    The Baptist Vision
    Conclusion

Chapter 7—Practices: Actualizing Resources of the Vision | 90
    Introduction
    Social Practices
    Christ and Power
        Powerful Practices
        Preaching as a Powerful Practice
    Conclusion

Chapter 8—Reading the Bible in Community | 103
    Introduction
    The Question of Communal Hermeneutics
    Practices of Reading the Bible
    Conclusion

Chapter 9—Preaching, Church, and University | 117
    Introduction
    Three Sermons in a Worship Service: Present, Past, and Future
    Preaching in Educational Space
        Church and University in Paradox
        The Discipline of Homiletics
        From Conflict to Partnership: The Way to Mutual Understanding
    Conclusion

Conclusion | 135

    Bibliography | 141

Foreword

IN RECENT YEARS, THE eyes of the English-speaking world have become aware in a fresh and vibrant way of developments which have taken place in baptistic communities of the old Russian Empire. Fresh research on Johann G. Kargel, Gottfried Alf, and Vasily Pashkov have helped us see the theological formation of baptistic communities within the Russian Empire. Now, to add to this understanding, another generation of scholars is exploring theological, ecclesiological, and missional formations during the Soviet Empire, and indeed in the independent states which have emerged from the collapse of the Union of Soviet Socialist Republics in the early 1990s.

Prior to that and beyond the borders of the Soviet Empire, the global north had only a limited understanding of the virtues and practices of the oft-persecuted baptistic communities, which continued to exist, and in many cases develop, despite the best efforts of Joseph V. Stalin, Nikita S. Kruschev, Leonid I. Brezhnev, and the Soviet politburo members to crush, suppress, and eliminate them.

Some knowledge of the real lives of these believing communities was possible through the valiant efforts of western Baptist leaders such as E. A. Payne, D. S. Russell, Denton Lotz, and Gerhaard Claas, who took every opportunity to get behind the Iron Curtain and meet baptistic believers. Today, the ecclesial life, work, worship, and mission of these baptistic communities over the course of a century has become accessible to us by western authors such as Walter Sawatsky, Mary Raber, Heather J. Coleman, Sheryl Corrado, Albert W. Wardin, and Gregory L. Nichols, who have immersed themselves in the life of the churches of Russia and its satellite nations to bring the history, theology, mission, and community life of eastern European baptistic communities to us in fresh and stimulating ways. Now we understand better the work and theology of the likes of Johann (Ivan) Kargel, Martin Kalweit, Vasily A. Pashkov, and others.

Even more importantly, to my mind, we have now raised up a generation of younger scholars from Russia, Ukraine, Lithuania, Kazakhstan, Estonia, and elsewhere who grew up in the old Soviet Empire as believers in these baptistic communities and are now devoting themselves to the task of understanding, analyzing, and offering respectable and authentic accounts of the life and nature of the believers' churches during a period of repression and persecution to a wider readership. Lina Toth (nee Andronovienė), Toivo Pilli, Meego Remel, Constantine Prokhorov, Leonid Mikhovich, Alexander Popov, Sergei Sannikov, and others have deeply enriched our appreciation of believing communities in the local setting through their dedicated research and publications.

Timofey (Tima) Cheprasov is another of this younger generation of able scholars. He grew up in a Baptist home in Voronezh in Russia and was baptized into the church. Having a skill with languages, he played a crucial role in the development of a school of preaching, formed at the request of the Russian Baptist leadership by the International Baptist Theological Seminary (then based in Prague) in 1999, and which worked out of Bryansk in Southwest Russia under the inspired leadership of David M. Brown, a member of the IBTS faculty and an authority on preaching. The book developed out of that preaching school, *Transformational Preaching*, continues to be widely used as a textbook in Russia. It was translated from David's English manuscript by Tima. David's influence and encouragement led Tima to study at IBTS in Prague, where he gained a Master's degree in theology and later a Doctorate, on which this book is based.

For Tima, an important question has been how the church in Russia has been formed and shaped over the past one hundred years by the weekly exposition of the word in the main Sunday service. The common practice amongst most Baptist communities in Russia has been (and for many it still is) to have three sermons preached in the principal two-hour act of worship. This exposure to preaching has been formative in shaping believing communities. He has experienced firsthand, week by week, the worship and preaching of a Russian Baptist church, but in his research he has sought the help of others—fellow students at IBTS, churches in Russia by both quantitative and qualitative research to explore the relationship between the preaching ministry and the virtues and practices of the communities in which the preaching takes place.

Tima seeks to explore the identity of local Russian Baptist communities based on his own experience, research, and mature reflection on the present realties. This is not a comprehensive work of history of Russian Baptists. Others have been engaged in that task. It is, however, a vitally important investigation of how believing communities are formed and shaped by their practices and not by the pronouncement of the Moscow-based leadership.

Tima begins this work by examining the Stundists, a group in the time of Imperial Russia who explored the Bible in a way which ultimately caused them to be expelled from the Russian Orthodox Church and form one of the streams of life leading to the evangelical baptistic communities, which gained strength and importance in the communist era.

Orthodoxy is built into the Russian spiritual community, so the key theological and spiritual movements in orthodoxy inevitably had an influence upon baptistic communities; Tima picks out several key themes of theosis, sobornost, and charismatic preaching to reflect on the way baptistic communities developed. Another major influence was clearly that of the oppressive Soviet regime which, in many periods over the past one hundred years, took a particular dislike to these evangelical movements. The political restrictions on activities and the continuing underlying threat of persecution affected styles of preaching and the nature of the spirituality which was espoused from the pulpit.

All of this sets a comprehensive scene for the challenge of the present day as baptistic communities live with new freedoms and recognition, younger believers enjoy educational opportunities, and the churches are forced to look afresh at preaching styles, the place of theological education, and the development of hermeneutical tools, which take account of theological and biblical knowledge, which was previously closed off to them.

There are many challenges in this, but Tima effectively uses the notion of the late Jim McClendon that intentional convictional communities of belief have powerful practices which shape who they are and how they cohere. This book opens up, in a remarkable way, important aspects of Russian baptistic life at the grassroots. Beyond that, it also provides vital material for reflection and subsequent action by those who engage in the work of ministerial formation in a wider context. Nevertheless, it is but a stage on a journey towards understanding. The journey itself is vital as a

Foreword

new generation of Russian Baptists grows up educated in a different way and in the context of a globalized digital world which, unless we are all very careful, the convictional communities of baptistic belief may seem a marginal distraction.

This is a book worth studying diligently as we seek to be vital, faithful people in this current postmodern age.

Keith G. Jones
President, the Baptist Historical Society
Rector, IBTS Prague, 1998–2013

Acknowledgments

"Dad, look how far I can throw a stone!" Alexey, my five-year old son, was preparing to hurl a pebble into the lake on our weekend away in the Lake District in Cumbria. Of course, the stone did not go particularly far, but it produced a surprisingly big splash, causing ripples—in otherwise perfectly still water—to spread for many meters in all directions, and even alarming a family of wild geese that was floating near the shore. At that moment Alexey could not imagine that he had helped me finalize the title for this book on preaching in Russian Baptist churches and its often unnoticed—yet significant with respect to their life and ministry—consequences, just like a small rock causes disturbances disproportionate to its size.

As I finish writing the last remaining pages of this book, which began as a PhD research project nearly twelve years ago, I want to express my appreciation and deep gratitude to everyone who has assisted me through their advice, challenging questions, recommendations, encouragement, and inspiration.

First of all, I would like to say thank you to the community of International Baptist Theological Seminary in Prague. Every research colloquium was a massive inspiration for me. I am very grateful to all the tutors and students for their input into my project. Being part of the residential community in Prague has deeply affected the way I understand both academic work and Christian ministry, and I feel privileged to have had this experience.

I would like to express special gratitude to David Brown, Keith Jones, and Parush Parushev. These people have introduced me to theological

Acknowledgments

studies and academic research. They have encouraged me to take on this project. This work would have never been completed without their priceless advice, guidance in my research, and encouragement.

I greatly appreciate the support of Bury Baptist Church, our church family over the past six years, who allowed me to have time to finish my PhD thesis, and then work on this book.

I am thankful to my parents, for their assistance and encouragement, and to my sons, Alexey and Daniel, who, apart from their contribution to the title, have patiently waited for their father to "finish his book without pictures." And last, but not least, I want to express my deepest gratitude to my wife, Yulia. Her encouragement, inspiration, and patience are impossible to overestimate.

Abbreviations

ARUEC	All-Russia Union of Evangelical Christians
AUCECB / VSEKHB	the All-Union Council of Evangelical Christians-Baptists (in Russian Vsesoyuznii Sovet Evangelskikh Khristian-Baptistov)
BCC	Bible Correspondence Courses
BV	Bratskii Vestnik [The Herald of the Brotherhood]
CECB	The Congress of Evangelical Christians - Baptists
ECB	Evangelical Christians-Baptists
GULAG	Glavnoie Upravleniie Lagerei [Main Camp Administration]
MTSECB	Moscow Theological Seminary of Evangelical Christians-Baptists
RUECB	the Russian Union of Evangelical Christians-Baptists
TCMII	Training Christians for Ministry (TCM) International Institute (USA, Austria)

Translation and Transliteration

Whenever Russian sources are quoted, all the translation work from Russian into English is done by me, unless specified otherwise.

The English language quotations of the Bible come from the New International Version. Russian Synodal version is used for all biblical quotations which are translated from Russian.

I am using the established English spellings of common Russian names and terms, as found in common dictionaries. Other Cyrillic words are transliterated by the following system:

А – A	И – I
Б – B	Й – I
В – V	К – K
Г – G	Л – L
Д – D	М – M
Е – E	Н – N
Ё – IE	О – O
Ж – ZH	П – P
З – Z	Р – R

Translation and Transliteration

С – S	Щ – SHCH
Т – Т	Ъ – "
У – U	Ы – Y
Ф – F	Ь – '
Х – KH	Э – E
Ц – TS	Ю – IU
Ч – CH	Я – IA
Ш – SH	

Preface

THE MAJORITY OF CHURCHES of Evangelical Christians – Baptists[1] in Russia have one distinctive feature: the role of preaching in the worship service. Each service contains at least three twenty- to forty-minute sermons. Time-wise, about three quarters of a two-hour service is devoted to preaching the word. Therefore, for all who grew up in a Russian Baptist church or visited it at least occasionally, the question "what is preaching?" will be answered quickly—it is the word of God. "How does preaching happen?" A member of the church comes up into the pulpit, reads a passage from the Bible and then shares his[2] thoughts on it. Similarly the question "why preaching?" is also easily answered: the proclamation of the word of God produces faith in its listeners. Such a response is an allusion to Romans 10:17, which in the Russian Synodal Translation says, "Faith is from hearing and hearing is from the Word of God." Traditionally this is used as a reference to preaching—the proclaimed word.

Thus preaching is seen as something very powerful for forming convictions of the listeners, for making Christians more Christlike, and ultimately for making them better Baptists. The question that is never asked

---

1. Throughout this work, unless specified otherwise, the phrase *Russian Baptists* is a reference to the communities and believers that are part of the Russian Union of Evangelical Christians – Baptists (RUECB).

2. Habitually, women are barred from preaching, despite the fact that in the past the official position of the Baptist Union allowed women to preach. Although there was no official statement prohibiting women from this ministry, at present the idea of female preachers is opposed, as it is generally understood to be against the teaching of the Bible. For more on women in ministry, see chapter 3.

PREFACE

though is whether this assumption, of preaching possessing great formative power, is a correct one. Thus the lack of critical analysis of the role of preaching defines the main objective for this research: to analyze whether Russian Baptists' presupposition that preaching is a major driving force in forming Baptist identity is a correct one, and thus concluding whether it rightly holds its position of high respect and reverence.

Paradoxically, there is little work done on this subject. The absence of written sources does not imply that the question of preaching has been neglected, yet due to the high view of this practice, with heavy emphasis on the work of the Holy Spirit in the act of proclamation, most articles on preaching and preachers have focused primarily on the qualities of preachers and predominantly their spiritual preparation for the act of proclamation. There was no effort made to engage in the critical assessment of actual convictions that both preachers and listeners held about preaching, how these convictions developed, and most importantly whether preaching rightly held the central position among all other church activities. Furthermore, an attempt to perform such an assessment would be considered inappropriate, if not sinful.

Similarly, little help can be received from books and articles published in the English-speaking world. Unlike a few aspects of Russian Baptist ecclesiology—such as charity work, spirituality, and history, that did draw some research interest—preaching, despite its obvious importance for the life of the communities of faith, has never attracted much attention from pastors, missionaries, and educators who visited the Soviet Union (USSR) after the fall of the Iron Curtain. The neglect can be explained, and to a certain degree justified, if one tries to assess the often poorly translated and nonlinear sermons through the lens of Anglo-American homiletical tradition. For example, Harris speaks about Russian preaching as a low-quality product of a culture that had never had democracy, and therefore had a poor history of public speaking.[3] Henceforth, Russian Baptist preaching was perceived as something that required correction and modification either through training or example, but not as something that deserved attention on its own.

Nevertheless, this position misses the point that preaching in Russia has never been viewed as a public speech developed according to some

3. However, considering his rather superficial understanding of the historical, cultural, and theological milieu of Russian Baptist churches and their practices, his article should be seen as a foreigner's impressions rather than an academic study of any sort. (Harris, "Toward an Understanding.")

PREFACE

laws of rhetoric. I hope to fill in this gap with my work, by looking at the history of the development of preaching in Russian Baptist churches and the theology behind it. However, in saying that Russian preaching should be viewed within its context, that it deserves to be studied on its own right, I do not imply that whatever is pronounced from Russian Baptist pulpits has to be highly valued, and that no improvements are possible. On the contrary, unfortunately there is much low-quality preaching (whatever view of preaching is upheld!) taking place. Paying tribute to the past and respecting the heritage are not sufficient reasons to neglect the importance of revisiting even the most respected and valued practices of a Christian community. Development and growth begins with critical analysis, with the ability to see both strengths and weaknesses. This is a difficult process, since such study inevitably penetrates dearly held convictions of communities and individual believers.

Despite a call to developing a critical instrument for assessment of the practice of proclamation, I do not start with the presupposition that Russian preaching has failed and thus requires correction. My primary goal is to see how preaching is understood, how it has developed, and how it fits into the convictions of Russian Baptists. In a way this is a question: What role does preaching play in making Russian Baptists who they are? And, finally, does preaching continue to develop together with the church that has undergone great changes in recent years?

Let me offer a brief overview of this book. The first five chapters are an inquiry into the question of Russian Baptist ecclesial identity and the role of preaching (as one of their major practices and characteristic features) in forming, preserving, and passing on this identity. Identity is understood as a way of communal living, which includes individual ethics, but also goes beyond it. Chapters 1–4 will mostly concentrate on questions of historical development of Russian baptistic[4] churches and their preaching, and the context in which they've existed. It has to be noted that historical material in these chapters is organized thematically, with each of these topics (such

---

4. I use the term "Baptist" to refer to the congregations which define themselves as Baptists, and which is reflected in their name. The term "baptist" or "baptistic" (with a lower case "b") is a reference to a wider tradition, which includes Molokans, Mennonites, Brethren, Pentecostals, Evangelical, or Gospel Christians—those who share "some or all of those values associated with believer's baptism, the autonomy of the local congregation and freedom of conscience" (Wright, *Free Church, Free State*, xxiii). For the origin of the terms, see McClendon, *Ethics*, 2nd ed., 19; and Grams and Parushev, *Towards an Understanding*, 10.

as cultural and theological contexts of preaching and development of baptistic educational institutions) developed historically.

The rather extensive presentation of the historical material as well as the analysis of the cultural and religious context is necessary, since it highlights the connections between the ways preaching was understood and practiced and the effect it produced on the ecclesial life of the communities. Nonetheless, this is not a comprehensive history of the Baptist movement. Rather, the historical part of my work is an attempt to retell the story of Russian baptistic communities through the lens of the development of their ministry of proclamation.[5]

Chapter 1 shows the important role preaching played in the formation of the first baptistic groups in the Russian Empire. Using Stundists as an example, I will argue that the ability to read the Bible and the desire to interpret it within the community of believers caused excommunication of these believers from the Orthodox Church. Thus it was preaching in a form of retelling a biblical story with simple explanation and application that became one of the main driving forces behind the emergence of the baptistic communities.

Chapter 2 deals with questions of context. It would be naïve to assume that Russian baptists, being a tiny minority in a country where Orthodox spirituality and ethics penetrated all areas of social life, could have developed their theology and practice without any influence from the Orthodox Church. As I offer a brief overview of Orthodox concepts of theosis, sobornost, and charismatic preaching, a number of striking similarities with the way preaching is understood and practiced in contemporary Baptist churches will allow better understanding of various convictions related to preaching and worship.

Chapters 3 and 4 attempt to build a paradigm of the development of baptistic preaching in Russia. The oppressive and hostile environment

---

5. It is necessary to point out that I do not deal with Pentecostal churches, communities that belong to the Council of Churches of Evangelical Christians-Baptists, or any other denominations, which were part of the All-Union Council of Evangelical Christians-Baptists (AUCECB) during the Soviet time, but which exist as independent ecclesial bodies. Due to the limitations of this work I chose to focus specifically on churches that currently form the Russian Union of Evangelical Christians–Baptists (RUECB). These limitations provide a clarifying point for a rather brief overview of several important and controversial issues in the history of the AUCECB, particularly its forceful merger with Pentecostal communities in 1945, and the split in the AUCECB of 1961, resulting in the appearance of the Council of Churches. Whilst these are extremely important events in the history of the baptistic movement, they are outside the scope of my research.

in which these communities existed produced a distinct imprint on their preaching—it became over-spiritualized, with heavy emphasis placed on the spirituality of the preachers as the most important prerequisites for a successful sermon. Eventually, this gave preachers, and particularly the leadership of churches, special positions of authority, thus bringing issues of power into the realm of homiletics.

Chapter 5 addresses the present state of preaching in Russian Baptist churches. I introduce the stage where preaching takes place, and answer the question of what preaching is currently understood and expected to be, as well as present the immediate context for preaching—the worship service[6]—and address the question of who is allowed to preach.

In this analysis of the origins and contemporary state of baptistic preaching I will highlight an important point: throughout their history, Russian baptists dealt with preaching solely as ministry, primarily consisting of preparatory (rational and spiritual) and proclamatory parts (the delivery of a sermon with all the elements such as the role of the Holy Spirit, the preacher, and the listeners being taken into consideration). Depending on the resources available, or the political environment around the church, the emphasis on the most important elements of preaching changed. The more professional approach in terms of knowledge of theology, hermeneutics, and rhetoric that developed at the beginning of the twentieth century, during the time of fast church growth, was replaced by a period of survival when the spirituality of the preachers was emphasized even at the expense of rational preparation of a sermon. Still, in essence the approach to preaching remained the same: mere acts of proclamation, with some educational and spiritual power. Various schools and educational programs that sprung up during the 1990s and 2000s continued this trend.

Such a reductionist approach, as it will be shown, is bound to create difficulties. Various unsuccessful[7] educational projects, as well as generally

---

6. Throughout this work I use the term "worship" in a simple way, referring to a church gathering with the purpose of praising God and experiencing him through singing, praying, and listening to the proclaimed word. Such utilization of the word does not imply that I reject other existing views. The usage is a matter of convenience, since I focus on those practices of the community of believers that, when taken together, are commonly known as "corporate worship" or a "worship service."

7. When addressing such subjects as preaching or teaching preaching, a definition of success enters a subjective area of individual expectations (of teachers, students, and churches, as recipients of the end product) and various theological convictions (what the measure of success is depends heavily on how preachers and their listeners understand theirs and God's work in the world and in the church). Nevertheless, the use of the

accepted *poor* quality of preaching, yet surprising lack of critical stance in local churches towards its preaching and preachers proves this point. I will argue that unless preaching is understood and taught as a *practice* rather than a mere rhetorical skill, it will be hard to open the way for further growth. Employing the concept of powerful practices as developed by McClendon, I will point out that when teaching or evaluating preaching, its success should not be measured based solely on listeners' perception of separate acts of proclamation. Rather its practitioners need to be aware of the constructive potential and hidden destructive forces of the ministry they aspire to develop.

Following Wright's argument that understanding "who I am" is an important question, which has to be answered prior to "how I should live," I will attempt to outline the constants that constitute and define the Russian Baptist church.[8] Hence the subject of baptistic identity[9] and practices that enhance and develop that identity, and the role of preaching amongst these practices, will be the focus of chapters 6–8.

Chapter 9 will bring this study of preaching into the educational institution. Since 1989, when the first theological school in USSR was opened in Odessa (Ukraine), seminaries, Christian universities, Bible schools, and distance-learning courses have been playing a more prominent role in the preparation of pastors, missionaries, and even lay preachers. However, the way the subject of preaching is approached and taught, when little or no attention is paid to the role and place of proclamation in the formation of baptistic identity, hampers the potential effect their graduates can make and does not provide them with a tool to understand the environment they

---

word "unsuccessful" is deliberate. Much of contemporary preaching in Russian Baptist churches can only be characterized as low quality from both rhetorical and theological perspectives. Nevertheless, it is still not uncommon to hear dismissive remarks about theological education in general and preachers' training in particular. Thus, even though various training programs have produced quality preachers, the impact of these programs is limited to their graduates, with the majority of churches and pastors still not showing their support of theological education, which is clearly seen in the lack of financial support and declining numbers of prospective students.

8. Wright, *New Baptists, New Agenda*, 11.

9. Rather than attempting to explore all possible ways of defining the concept of identity, I use it in relation to something that makes a person or a community part of one culture (in this case, a baptistic culture), that makes them distinct from others, that sets the direction for their existence and defines their practices (McClendon and Smith, *Convictions*, 91) Thus, speaking about identity and identity formation, I address the question, of how certain convictions are being formed.

are intending to minister in. My hope is that this project will offer a critical tool that educational institutions could use to enhance their understanding of the practice of preaching and the approach they use in teaching.

Finally, it is necessary to set the limits to this research. I will first of all focus on preaching as a practice, and those convictions that are related to this practice. The content of preaching, though occasionally referred to, will not be paid too much attention. This neglect is deliberate, since the limitations of this work will not allow me to address all the aspects of the ministry of proclamation. It is my hope that this study may serve as a stimulus for further research and development in the area of homiletics and its role and place in the life of baptistic churches in Russia.

1

Retelling the Story
The Beginning of the Russian Baptistic Movement[1]

Introduction

A NUMBER OF BOOKS on the history of the Russian Baptist movement begin with a description of the religious scene of the Russian Empire. Their authors, particularly if they come from the baptistic tradition, often seek to make a case for the indigenous roots of the movement. Thus, they refer to the existence of such groups as Dukhobors, Khlysts, Skoptses, and Molokans, arguing that for centuries the peoples of Russia[2] were involved in a spiritual quest of a sort, with Baptists being a natural outcome of this pilgrimage.[3] However, whilst some of these groups, like Molokans, do show obvious connections to at least one of the first Baptist centers (in the Caucasus), most of the abovementioned sects had little or nothing in common with Baptists. They existed and coexisted far earlier than the first signs

---

1. The materials of this chapter were published in an article in Cheprasov, "Political and Religious Factors," 46–58.

2. Using the phrase "Russian people," I refer to the various ethnic groups who lived within the territory of the Russian Empire. Such use is out of mere convenience. I neither imply that there was one ethnicity nor try to deprive other nations and ethnicities of their history.

3. Coleman suggests that from the very beginning the Baptist movement in Russia struggled with the accusations of being a German faith, which inevitably raised questions of their political loyalty. Taking into account two wars during which the Russian Empire and the Soviet Union fought with Germany, the proof of their indigenous origin was crucial for their survival. (Coleman, "Most Dangerous Sect," ch. 1)

of Baptists in Russia can be traced. Moreover, most of these religious groups were formed around a particular charismatic leader (or several leaders).[4] None became a movement that received recognition and support across the country. And it was only in the second half of the nineteenth century when evangelicals like Stundists, Paskovites[5], and Baptists began to stir minds and cause controversies in different corners of the empire. These dissenters from the Orthodox Church were constantly persecuted; nonetheless their numbers grew rapidly, counting tens of thousands of active members in only twenty years.[6]

Albert Wardin argues that while multiple factors need to be considered in order to explain the quick spread of the Baptist movement over the vast territory of the Russian Empire—sociological, political, and religious situation in the country; the financial support, evangelistic and educational efforts of German Baptists and Mennonites; and the passion and zeal of laypersons and homegrown evangelists in spreading the teaching—all of these factors are secondary, pointing to the indigenous roots of the movement.[7]

Without rejecting the contribution of Christians from abroad, I wish to concentrate on the indigenous elements in the origins of the baptistic movement in Russia. I will argue that a thaw in state internal politics and control allowed freer thinking in society. This and the serious crisis that the Orthodox Church was going through, resulted in a radical movement within the church. This movement grew out of a desire to bring a positive change into the established church, and to a large extent was a result of communal interpretation of the Bible. The politics of persecution that both civil officials and the Orthodox clergy had acquired forced these radicals to split and form a new denomination. One of the major marks of this denomination was preaching. Thus my claim is that preaching played a formative role in establishing and spreading the baptistic movement. It is important to emphasize that this preaching had a particular

---

4. For further reading on these movements, see Michels, *At War with the Church*, and Paert, *Old Believers, Religious Dissent*. A helpful perspective can be found in Katunskii, *Staroobriadchestvo*, 39–40.

5. *Pashkovites*, also known as *Evangelical Christians*, has a particular meaning in Russia. This is a baptistic movement that began in the 1870s and was associated with the names of Lord Radstock, an English lay evangelist, who made several trips to Russia to preach among nobility, and Colonel Vasilii Pashkov, a wealthy aristocrat, who became a passionate evangelical preacher and a leader of the movement of Evangelical Christians.

6. Fetzer, "Baptists in Russia," 126.

7. Wardin, "Penetration of Baptists," 47.

form—retelling Biblical narrative in understandable language with an immediate unsophisticated application.

Russian Empire in the Second Half of the Nineteenth Century

The second half of the nineteenth century was marked by a set of unique prerequisites, making Russian society fertile soil for the emergence of the baptistic movement. First, although the reforms of Alexander II did not change the country's political system—an absolute monarchy with strict control of all spheres of social life—they still resulted in far greater political, social, and religious freedoms than any other era of Russian imperial history. Second, the crisis that struck the Orthodox Church at that time prompted many people to look for other forms of religious expression. Although it would be wrong to suggest that the people started searching for an alternative denomination or religion, there was a great desire to see changes within the established church. And last but not least, the fact that for the first time in history the Bible was published in contemporary Russian language and was made widely available, allowed people to further explore Christian faith for themselves.

Freedom

The rule of Emperor Nicolas I ended in 1856 leaving the country facing complete catastrophe. Failure in foreign politics and serious internal economic problems caused disillusionment in the ideas of Russia's uniqueness and superiority, resulting in an epistemological crisis of a sort.[8] The loss in the Crimean War, and the subsequent destruction of Russia's military prestige and political influence, not only dealt a blow to national pride, but also provided impetus for reforms.[9] Alexander II appeared to be the answer to that need. Although his life tragically ended with his assassination, his reign could be identified as one of the most important periods in Russian history. His reforms were incomplete and could not untie the knot of the country's social and economic problems, with perhaps tragic consequences.

---

8. I am referring to MacIntyre's concept of a crisis of self-perception that changes the course of social life, being caused by a certain discovery or event. ("Epistemological Crises, Dramatic Narrative," 138–39)

9. Freeze, "Reform and Counter Reform," 172.

Still the impact of Alexander II, Tsar-Liberator, whose rule is known as the Epoch of Great Reforms, cannot be overestimated.

One of the most needed changes was related to the institution of serfdom—a form of slavery that was beginning to threaten the stability of the country. The process of freeing the serfs was initiated in 1857 with the work of the Committee on Peasant Reform. Public discussions were initiated, bringing the social problems, which were already highly criticized in progressive literature, into focus for the whole country. The process concluded in 1861 when all the serfs were freed and given the possibility to buy land allotments and transfer them into private or communal property.[10]

Without describing all the complexities of the reform, it is sufficient to say that the peasants were left with the feeling that they were robbed of freedom, since their expectations of receiving land and economic independence were not met. They became poorer than before—freedom brought hunger. This dissatisfaction resulted in numerous violent revolts.[11] Former serf-owners were similarly frustrated. They lost their power without receiving compensation; they were short of finances and lacked prospects for the future, struggling with adjustment to a changing social reality.[12] As several historians note, despite the fact that the reforms had transformed the country, it became one of the major reasons for the Revolution of 1918.[13]

Gradual relaxation of censorship was another important element of freedom. Soon after censorship was changed from precensorship to postcensorship with much weaker control, a lot of earlier prohibited literature was published, introducing new philosophical, social, and religious ideas onto the public scene.[14] Education also underwent a significant change with many new schools being opened across the country. Universities[15] received "greater rights for its teaching staff and even some recognition of student rights."[16] These freedoms caused rapid expansion of philosophical thought and increased political activism among the people. The wider society did

---

10. Riasanovsky and Steinberg, *History of Russia,* 344.

11. Freeze, "Reform and Counter Reform," 177.

12. The inability of nobility to adapt to the changing socioeconomic realities is well depicted in a famous play by Chekhov called *Vishnevii Sad (The Cherry Orchard).*

13. Vernadsky, *History of Russia,* 159–69.

14. See Black, *Transformation of Russian Society.*

15. The term "university" is used in two ways. In chapters 1 and 3, the term is used in relation to any institution of higher education. In chapter 9, the term is a reference to Christian educational institutions.

16. Freeze, "Reform and Counter Reform," 178.

not always welcome these new developments. Universities became known as places of liberal thinking, nests of atheism and ungodliness, and even as producers of revolutionaries and rebels.[17]

As a consequence of the abovementioned factors, as well as major administrative and judicial reform, there appeared a new social class—*raznochintsy*.[18] The core of this group was the growing educated middle class: doctors, engineers, scientists, writers, publishers, journalists. The group expanded in size and in its social importance. Ironically, this new class, which was in many ways a result of the Great Reforms, despised both the reforms and the government, demanding complete transformation of the country.[19]

Nevertheless, this general dissatisfaction with the existing order and the belief that the reforms were incomplete also brought positive outcomes. One of them was a populist movement based upon a belief that it was possible to achieve the transformation of the society through education and the enlightenment of the masses. Heier wrote,

> The movement reached its peak in 1873–74 when thousands, not only of young men and women, but also of men in well-established professions, (including hundreds of aristocrats) roamed the Russian countryside, often dressed as peasants, to carry out their enlightening propagandist activities. They abandoned the universities and life of comfort in order to serve the people and be one with them in spirit.[20]

However, peasants turned out to be the most conservative social group. They neither accepted these "western things" nor the people who were trying to "enlighten" them. Police archives hold multiple accounts of peasants' reports on the activities of the populists.

---

17. The struggles and despair of the poor students was illustrated by Fyodor Dostoyevsky in the person of Rodion Raskolnikov, the main character of the novel *Crime and Punishment*.

18. "Raznochintsy" is a complex word that consists of two roots—"raznii" (different) and "chin" (social status)—with the literal meaning of a mixture of people of different social groups.

19. Nihilism was one of its extreme manifestations. The movement was popular among the educated youth and, although not revolutionary in its focus, it was marked by a rejection of absolute values and belief in the absolute power of science. (Heier, *Religious Schism*, 6)

20. Heier, *Religious Schism*, 6–7; also Ovsianiko-Kulikovskii, "'Kaiushchiesia Dvoriane,'" 83–99.

This period of Russian history presents a fascinating mosaic of new philosophical ideas and attempts to implement and translate them into reality. It was a time that many historians call "The Russian Enlightenment," which significantly changed and influenced the development of the country. Nevertheless, despite all the newness, freedom, and openness, or perhaps because of it, one of the major results of this time was a deeply divided society.

The Crisis

Without any doubt, in the second half of the nineteenth century Russian society was in a spiritual crisis. The educated intelligentsia and nobility were seeking answers in science. The uneducated peasants turned to the church, which itself needed help. The beginning of the crisis that struck the Russian Orthodox Church can be traced to the time of Peter I. One of his numerous reforms was the replacement of the influential figure of a patriarch with Most Holy Governing Synod, a new governing body which was presided over by a civil official, the Chief Procurator. This marked the change from the church being the heart of the nation into its becoming an institution, a "ministry of spiritual affairs" of a sort, which was gradually drifting away from the needs and struggles of the people.[21]

The state officials' approach to the church as an influential agent is best illustrated by the words of Dmitrii Tolstoi, Chief Procurator of the Holy Synod from 1865 to 1880, who described the role the church "as no more and no less than a force that must be subordinate to the government and of which a wise government can make clever use for its own ends."[22] Therefore, the bureaucrats were never shy of displaying its concern for the "well-being" of the church in rather unexpected ways. As noted by Shevzov,

> State-initiated regulations during the eighteenth century made themselves felt in internal, even sacred, aspects of ecclesial life . . . In this vein, for instance, a 1774 directive delegated to local civil officials the responsibility of making sure that people attended church on Sundays and major feast days, thereby blurring the boundaries between civil and purely ecclesial life. A similar

---

21. Iswolsky, *Christ in Russia*, 113.
22. Feoktistov, *Vospominaniia*, 169.

blurring of boundaries was evident in civil legislation mandating annual confession and Communion.[23]

Thus entering a time of social unrest, a time of disillusionment, and spiritual search for the meaning of life by many people, the church needed help itself. Its clergy were unable (and to a certain degree uninterested in trying) to understand and help people. Its witness, ethical life, and teaching were almost nonexistent due to corruption caused by poverty, poor education, and a nearly total lack of support given to local parish priests. The rites and liturgy of the church seemed inadequate and unclear to peasants and were considered irrelevant by the nobility and intelligentsia.[24] Not surprisingly, one of the key reforms of Alexander II was related to the church, focusing on developing a number of initiatives in the areas of education, parish management, and fundraising.[25] Paradoxically, it was exactly such intrusive "care" that instigated the abovementioned crisis and caused clergy's refusal to conform to the reforms,[26] for they saw that the church "was kept like a captive under the pretext of its own safety."[27]

In the second half of the nineteenth century both society and the established church were struggling with serious issues, looking for new ways of development, and realizing the need for a change. It was an age of disillusionment with the "kind Tsar" working for the freed serfs, and disappointment in socialist ideas among the wide spectrum of intelligentsia, some of whom turned to terrorism; it was an age of either cynicism or the rise of conservative ideas among the aristocracy. That was a time when the guidance of the church was especially needed but was missing.[28]

23. Shevzov, *Russian Orthodoxy on the Eve*, 17.

24. At the beginning of the twentieth century, Sergei Margaritov, a Russian Orthodox priest, argued that the failure of the Orthodox Church to provide guidance for the freed serfs, and the uncontrolled reading and interpretation of the Bible by the laity, were among the main reasons for the appearance and spread of the baptistic movements in Russia. (*Istoriia russkikh misticheskikh i ratsionalisticheskikh sect*, 147–48)

25. Freeze, "Reform and Counter Reform," 180.

26. Polunov, "Church, Regime, and Society," 34.

27. Heier, *Religious Schism*, 17.

28. It would be an exaggeration to say that the disillusionment in the role and place of the Orthodox Church in society (Heier, *Religious Schism*, ch. 1) became the reason for the rise of the baptistic movement. The whole society was so deeply Orthodox that people could not see a viable alternative, and could not imagine a different way of life. Later in this chapter, when looking at Stundists, I will point to the fact that neither Stundism nor Pashkovism began as an alternative to Orthodoxy. Rather, they were sincere attempts to bring about a positive change into the established church and wider society.

The Bible

The history of the Russian people receiving the printed Scripture began in 1816, when the Bible in Old Church Slavonic was published. The first 25,000 volumes of the Russian translation of the New Testament were printed in 1822. Unfortunately, the initiative to translate and publish the Bible at that time was not supported by the clergy. After the death of Alexander I, the Bible Society was closed and those New Testaments that were not distributed were burnt.

The second attempt at making the Bible widely available is connected to the name of Moscow Metropolitan Philaret (1782–1867). Under his influence the Holy Synod took a decision to translate the Bible into the then contemporary Russian language. Eighteen sixty-two was a crucial year for Russian Christianity. In that year the New Testament in contemporary language was published (the full Bible was published in 1876). In 1863, a small group began raising funds to assist people in purchasing Bibles. Three years later this group grew into the Society of Distribution of the Holy Scriptures.[29] The work of this and other organizations that were involved in the spread of the Scriptures was tremendous. During thirty years of this ministry they sold and distributed over 1.5 million copies of the New Testament, including 150,000 copies distributed in the Asian part of the empire. Many of these books were distributed by *colporteurs*, full-time traveling distributors of Bibles and other spiritual literature. They walked through towns and villages, carrying the books and the good news—sales were always coupled by simple preaching.[30]

The Stundist Dissent

Now I would like to turn the first Stundist communities: their beginning, characteristic features, and practices which caused their excommunication from the Orthodox Church. This was accompanied by persecutions from both the clergy and state officials, and led to the eventual formation of a new denomination. In this short study I deliberately omit the Stundist movement among German colonists, instead focusing on the first known communities of Ukrainian Stundists, and their most prominent characteristic feature—communal preaching.

---

29. Reshetnikov and Sannikov, *Obzor istorii*, 68–69.
30. Torbet et al., *History of the Baptists*, 321.

Retelling the Story

The first Stundists appeared in 1862 in Osnova, a village in southern Ukraine. The group met in the house of the village elder Mikhail Ratushnii.[31] They were labeled as "Ukrainian Stunda" due to their similarities with German Stundists, such as evening meetings for Bible study and extemporaneous prayer, as well as their exemplary moral living.[32] As Rozhdestvenskii puts it, "They did not pay attention to the theoretical side of faith, but they put to the front its practical moments—the desire to live according to the Scripture."[33] The members of the group were devout Orthodox believers who attended church services, diligently studied the Bible, and used it as a guide for their lives.[34]

The example of Ivan Ryaboshapka, one of the prominent baptistic leaders, shows that the Orthodox Church initially did not perceive Stundist preaching as spreading another denomination. A passionate evangelist, Ryaboshapka was arrested in 1867 and in 1878, being accused of heresy, but both times he was released after a visit to a local priest for instruction, confession, and communion.[35] The police could not find links between Stundists and German settlers, as the only books that were used in their gatherings were "printed by the Russian Orthodox publishing houses."[36] Thus, they reported, "Stundists are not a religious sect; they appear to be a social group that believes that the Bible is better to be read at home, rather than in a church, where its reading is difficult for them to understand. That is why they gather in homes, read the Gospels, and interpret it as they can."[37]

There were several important characteristics of this first Stundist group. First, it was an indigenous group that was formed around an educated individual in order to study the Scripture. According to Ratushnii's personal witness, he decided to invite people into his house and to explain to them what the Bible had to say on their life after a village meeting, where

---

31. Zhuk, *Russia's Lost Reformation*, 192.

32. Yarigin argues that the label "stunda" was invented by the Orthodox clergy to create an impression of the foreign origins of the movement in the eyes of simple peasants and, more importantly, of the authorities. For the same reason, there were attempts to link Stundists to the Peasant Wars of the sixteenth century (*Evangelskoie dvizheniie v Volgo-Viatskom regione*, 28).

33. Rozhdestvenskii, *Yuzhno-russkii stundism*, 1.

34. Ibid., 56–57.

35. Doronitsin, *Materiali dlia istorii*, 11.

36. Zhuk, *Russia's Lost Reformation*, 165.

37. Ibid., 64.

the local priest was not able to respond to people's queries.[38] Second, they did not try to offer an alternative to the Orthodox Church. It was an attempt to add to the church's existing practices something that people were lacking—relevant guidance for their daily living. This point could be strengthened by the fact that the priest in Osnova was Greek, and could not speak Russian. Thus how could he give the needed guidance? However, acting on some strange conviction, upon his arrival in this area, the cleric began prohibiting people from reading the Scripture in their homes.[39]

Stundists could have been considered as exemplary Orthodox believers, in view of their sincere faith, zeal for studying the Bible, and pious living. However, the priests could neither understand nor accept these new expressions of the Orthodox spirituality, and tried to suppress them, often seeking assistance from the police. Such actions caused the breakaway of these nonconformists, who were already dissatisfied with the official church, beginning to see it as idolatrous and false.[40] Naturally, they turned to the non-Orthodox ecclesial bodies for help, which became a beginning for the Baptist movement. Thus the third characteristic feature of the movement was its gradual turn to Mennonites and then later to Baptists.[41]

It might be necessary to further elaborate on this last point. The separation from the Orthodoxy began almost six years after the group started to meet for Bible study and prayer, and was neither the goal of Ratushnii nor a sign of growing German (or any other) influence. Wardin argued that German missionaries did not try to evangelize the Russian Orthodox population "until after the Stundist movement had started . . . If anything, Ukrainian Stundists will reach out to Baptists rather than Baptists reaching out to them."[42] The shift from Orthodox-Stundism to Baptist-Stundism started when Efim Tsymbal persuaded Abraham Unger, a Mennonite Brethren preacher, to carry out water baptism for him and several other converted peasants in 1869.[43] Tsymbal later baptized Ryaboshapka, who in 1871 baptized Ratushnii and forty-eight people from his group.[44]

---

38. Ibid., 166.

39. Rozhdestvenskii, *Yuzhno-russkii stundism*, 57.

40. Savinskii, *Istoriia evangelskikh khristian-baptistov*, 103.

41. Zhuk, *Russia's Lost Reformation*, 192. Also Margaritov, *Istoriia russkikh misticheskikh i ratsionalisticheskikh sect*, 85–86, 147–48.

42. Wardin, "How Indigenous was the Baptist," 34–35.

43. Ibid., 34–35.

44. Coleman, *Russian Baptists and Spiritual Revolution*, 16. Also Rozhdestvenskii,

The name of Johann Wieler should be mentioned at this point.[45] After 1869 he had developed close relationships with Ratushnii and other Stundists, counseling "them to withdraw entirely from the Orthodox Church and form their own congregations."[46] This prompted the transformation of Stundists as a radical Orthodox wing into independent baptistic communities. On November 28, 1871, Ratushnii informed Archbishop Dmitrii about their withdrawal from the Orthodox Church[47]; then they took the icons and crucifixes from their homes and left them by the local church building to mark the separation.[48]

Despite their newly gained non-Orthodox identity, the movement grew among the peasants, the most conservative of Russia's social groups. This can only be explained by the closeness of the new movement to the beliefs and worldviews of simple people. Unlike the efforts of populists, rejected by peasants as western influences, baptistic movements that had indigenous Orthodox roots and theology were able to offer a more relevant version of the church, provide moral guidance, down-to-earth spirituality, and a community where everyone could take an active role in prayer, reading the Bible, and worship.

Conclusion

Let me draw a brief conclusion. In this chapter I have attempted to map the nature of the Great Reforms of the second half of the nineteenth century in the Russian Empire. The reforms resulted in a shaken and transformed society with freer thinking, yet at the same time a society that was deeply divided at all levels—economic, social, and spiritual. Unfortunately, at that turning point the Orthodox Church was not able to provide either moral or

---

Yuzhno-russkii stundism, ch. 2.

45. Johann Wieler, a German Mennonite, played one of the leading roles in the formation of the Russian Baptist Union. Closely connected to J. Gerhard Oncken and German Baptists, Wieler started the first German-speaking Baptist church in Odessa in the late 1860s. At the beginning of the 1870s, he supported Stundists in their unsuccessful appeals to the emperor for greater religious freedom. Wieler was one of the main organizers and a chairman at the 1884 conference in Novo-Vasilievka, when the Russian Baptist Union was formed. Wieler was elected as the first president of the union. For further reading, see Dyck, "Molding the Brotherhood."

46. Wardin, "How Indigenous was the Baptist," 35.

47. Rozhdestvenskii, *Yuzhno-russkii stundism*, 108.

48. Savinskii, *Istoriia evangelskikh khristian-baptistov*, 115.

spiritual guidance for its people. This inability was partially compensated for by the Bible being translated into the contemporary Russian language and made available for people, who started to read it in private, but more frequently in small home groups.

Such communitarian reading of the Bible and preaching resulted in a distinct emphasis on the need of a pious life and certain convictions about faith, which enabled laypeople to take on the roles traditionally only available to the clergy (particularly biblical interpretation). All of this was perceived as threatening to the established church and, therefore, to the state, thus causing persecution of these Christians. However, instead of suppressing the movement, rejection and persecution triggered the formation of a new denomination. Therefore, it is possible to argue that it was the practice of reading the Bible in a community and preaching (in a form of retelling and simplistic interpretation of the biblical stories) that were the initial formative forces that helped to single out and establish the Russian Baptist movement.

Certainly, these are not the only components that resulted in the appearance and the spread of Russian Baptists. I have mentioned only a few, omitting other important influences such as the life and example of the German settlers, the sporadic contributions of missionaries of various sorts, and others. This omission was done for only one reason—all those additional elements, though important, did not produce significant results until the Bible and the ability to read it was given to the people.

2

Theological Nest of the Russian Orthodox Church

Introduction

THE PREVIOUS CHAPTER SHOWED the important role that reading the Bible in a community of believers had played at the beginning of the baptistic movement in Russia. Undoubtedly those few pages cannot provide comprehensive coverage for such a complex subject as the origins of a religious movement. Defining the historical identity of Russian Baptists is a complicated, if not an impossible, task. Historical works on the topic include a wide spectrum of ideas and perspectives ranging from emphasizing the crucial role of western evangelicals to an equally persuasive view that this was an indigenous movement, conceived and developed without any significant influences from outside Russian society.

Consequently, after long hours of reading and comparing various books, articles, and dissertations, a careful reader may end up in a state of confusion, deciding that the task of writing a comprehensive history of the baptistic origin in Russia is impossible to fulfill. Such statements may prove to be right as so far there is no theory that can accommodate all known aspects of the emergence of the Russian baptistic movement into a coherent system.[1] It would not be wrong to suggest therefore, that the wide spectrum of the existing positions provides only partial insight into the historical background of the movement, since similar to the Anabaptist polygenetic origins, the roots of the contemporary Russian Baptist movement should

1. Popov, "Evangelical Christians-Baptists," 31–32.

be seen in numerous movements, groups, leaders, and influences. And similar to the origins of Anabaptists, the emergence and the spread of all these "heresies," as the Orthodox Church named them, at a scale that the society had never experienced before, was triggered by the availability of the Bible to the masses. However, since many people were illiterate, preaching became a major way of spreading the biblical message.

Every baptistic community develops in unique sociopolitical and theological settings, resulting in the diversity of baptistic believers across the globe. Today, preaching in Russian Baptist churches differs from preaching in Germany, England, or North America. Most of the existing differences are due to the unique context in which Russian baptistic communities developed. Thus, an insight into a number of major influences is crucial for an understanding of preaching in Russia, and how it was shaped.

Konstantin Prokhorov, in his recent PhD dissertation "Russian Baptists and Orthodoxy, 1960–1990: A Comparative Study of Theology, Liturgy and Traditions," argued that Russian Baptists received a vast heritage from orthodoxy, which resulted in great similarities in theology and practice between these two seemingly different Christian traditions. Thus, in this chapter it would suffice to offer a brief overview of the Orthodox theological context in which baptistic communities were developing, limiting my attention to only three themes, which I believe are very significant when it comes to studying the subject of Russian Baptist preaching. These are *theosis*, *sobornost*, and *preaching* in the Orthodox Church (particularly the concept of charismatic preaching).

Theosis: The Way . . .

The following quotation from *Bratskii Vestnik (The Herald of the Brotherhood)*, the official journal of the Russian Baptist Union, may serve as a helpful introduction of the importance of Orthodox spirituality for the baptistic movement:

> Is it difficult for us to humble ourselves before the Lord and to consider ourselves as great sinners? We are all sinners. We are poor and lazy in obeying the will of God. How many commandments we do not fulfill and how many commandments we break! When we come before the face of God, first of all we need to ask for mercy, patience and forgiveness . . . A true Christian must weep about losing the image of God and constantly insulting Him with

our sins. He must weep about bearing a name of a Christian and yet not fulfilling the promises given at baptism, about following the earthly, without thinking about heaven and eternal life . . . May every one of us follow the way shown to us by the Lord Jesus Christ, and be lifted to the gates of the Heavenly Kingdom, and may none be stripped of the joy of the future life.[2]

The concept of theosis or deification is linked both to the understanding of salvation and personal following of the way of Christ. Theosis can be characterized as an all-powerful and all-sanctifying work of God's grace through the Holy Spirit, possible because of the inborn human ability for transformation. Thus starts the process of the transformation of each individual, the whole of humanity, and even the visible and invisible universe. It is a process in which the likeness of God the Father is reflected in his creation through the mediation of the incarnate Christ by the work of the Holy Spirit.[3] Archimandrite George argues that theosis is the purpose of human life, being declared in the first chapter of the Bible, "He (God) does not wish him (a human) simply to be a being with certain gifts, certain qualities, a certain superiority over the rest of creation, He wishes him to be a god by Grace."[4]

Orthodox theology recognizes two aspects of salvation—the positive and the negative. The negative is an indication of being free from the false state of life, which is caused by sin.[5] This is where salvation is understood from the perspective of atonement and forgiveness. The positive aspect of salvation is in sanctification and theosis, which is emphasized more than a negative one. Hence salvation is not only about forgiveness of sins, but first of all is a renewal of a human being and a restoration of God's image in him.[6] The important question is not "salvation from what," but "salvation for what."[7] It is a mystery of humans reaching perfection through faithfulness and worship, thus fulfilling God's plan for the universe.[8]

---

2. M. N., "Velika nagrada vasha na nebesakh," 12–13.

3. Bilaniuk, "Mystery of Theosis or Divinization," 347. Cf. Pelikan, "Orthodox Theology in the West," 164.

4. George, *Theosis*, 19.

5. Aghiorgoussis, "Theology and Experience of Salvation," 406.

6. Bartos, *Deification in Eastern Orthodox Theology*, 253.

7. Borovoy, "What is Salvation?" 41.

8. Thunberg, *Man and the Cosmos*, 51.

Theosis, therefore, is both the process of transformation and the goal of that process that involves God and humans, who are called to a holy living. That life must be lived within the Orthodox Church, which by itself becomes of paramount importance, since "everything in the Church leads to Theosis; the Holy Liturgy, the Mysteries, divine Worship, the Gospel sermon, the fasting; all of these lead to this one thing. The Church alone is the place of Theosis."[9] Although theosis begins with God, being his gift and something that people cannot achieve by themselves, regardless of their efforts, people must do their best pursuing certain features of character. These are humility, asceticism or rejection of personal desires, and ability to pray, which is something to be achieved but also the means by which all these qualities can be obtained.[10]

The meaning of the concept of theosis is difficult to overestimate, as its emphasis on the importance of personal perfection and gradual improvement of the whole society became an often-repeated theme in literary and sociopolitical works of the first half of the nineteenth century. It is of particular significance for proclamation, as preaching (together with other church practices) leads to theosis. Yet, this process happens neither through a logical argumentation, nor by appealing to reason or addressing important moral questions and problems that the listeners have to deal with. Such approaches are seen as "western influences" on Orthodox theology and considered deeply misleading. Archimandrite George wrote,

> Unfortunately, the spirit of moralism . . . basing the Christian life on moral improvement, had adversely influenced the piety and spirituality of Christians to a significant degree even here in our land. We often cease to pursue Theosis because of Western influences on our theology . . . It is often responsible for atheism and for many people's indifference towards the spiritual life, especially among the young.[11]

The following is understood to be a solution—instead of moralizing, preaching should lead people to theosis through imparting God's grace, which people can only experience as they give up their individualistic pursuits and selfish ways.[12] Thus, it is first of all the attitude with which people come to participate in a divine liturgy that enables them to grasp the

9. George, *Theosis*, 36.
10. Ibid., 45–53.
11. Ibid., 66.
12. Ibid., 71.

glimpses of God's kingdom or be turned further away from it. The listeners, therefore, must enter the act of proclamation (as well as the rest of worship) with humility and reverence.

Richard Jensen argues that rather than being directed at the listeners, preaching should be seen as "an instrument of divine presence," which allows Christ to come to the believers. Hence, the focus of preaching is not the change of human hearts, but a mediation of divine agency. "Preaching of this sort is sacramental in character—a means of grace. It is theosis in action."[13] Such an attitude does not allow critical assessment of the message, as the absence of experiencing God's grace, despite participation in the act of worship, first of all points to the wrong attitude of the worshipper.

Concluding this overview of the concept of theosis and its impact on preaching, the following convictions should be highlighted: God is at work in the act of worship and preaching. His ways are often a mystery for the participants. Yet when worshippers come with the right heart and mind, in a spirit of humility and self-rejection, the Spirit of God is allowed to do his work in the lives and hearts of the congregation, which is the only place where theosis can take place. This brings me to the next important concept—*sobornost*.

. . . Walked Together with Others (Sobornost)

Reaction to the growing popularity of Western philosophical ideas gave rise to a movement of Slavophiles, a conservative stream of Russian educated aristocracy and intellectuals, which found its reflection in literature, philosophy, and the theology of the Orthodox Church.[14] Some identify it as a beginning of indigenous philosophical thought, since in the first half of the nineteenth century "philosophy in Russia was a forbidden fruit, being persecuted as something harmful and totally alien" for society.[15] Such reactionary views were opposed by the emerging class of intelligentsia, who believed that in the process of the enlightenment of the country, the newest philosophical thought (primarily German) must be welcomed and embraced.[16] In turn, Ivan Kireyevskii, a philosopher and literary critic, who is considered one of the co-founders of the Slavophile movement, argued

13. Jensen, *Envisioning the Word*, 43.
14. See Parushev, "Romantické vlivy na počatku ruského," 64–83.
15. Polonskii, *Moi studencheskie vospominaniia*, 364.
16. Khorunjii, *Posle pereriva*, part 1.

that whilst the achievements of modern education and science cannot be neglected, Russian philosophy must be connected to Russian culture.[17] Slavophiles concluded

> that they need to seek out the ideal for the future development of humanity away from the western rationalism, political liberalism and economic capitalism. Instead, they looked for this ideal in peasant Christian Russia prior to the reforms of the Emperor Peter the Great.[18]

Thus, the movement was a reaction to an overemphasis on reason as a way to solve social problems, and its prevalence over faith and the tradition of the church.[19]

Even though the movement was secular in its essence, with laypeople as their key thinkers, the most prominent of whom were Kireyevskii and Alexey Khomyakov, they supported and affirmed Orthodoxy as an inseparable part of Russian culture, which provided "spiritual bonding" for the people.[20] According to Parush Parushev,

> Orthodox ecclesiology, with its stress on the authority of the local church as a gathering of the community of the faithful, provided him (Khomyakov) with the resources to meet the challenge of integrating the two opposing phenomena of freedom and unity... he describes this synthesis in his essay, *The Church is One*, by coining a theological term, *sobornost*.[21]

In this concept, Khomyakov was able to formulate an integral part or even the essence of Orthodox religiosity,[22] the "one word (that) contains in itself the whole creedal statement."[23]

According to Khomyakov, God's truth is beyond logical understanding, and is undiscoverable by reason,[24] since truth is an object of faith, even though faith does not contradict logic or reason. Humans possess both rational will and moral freedom to choose righteousness or sin. Salvation

---

17. Kireyevskii, *Polnoie sobranie sochinenii*, 27, 264, 254.
18. Parushev, "Romantické vlivy na počatku ruského," 66.
19. Florovsky, *Puti russkogo bogoslovia*, 328.
20. Parushev, "Romantické vlivy na počatku ruského," 66.
21. Ibid., 66.
22. Esaulov, "Sobornost v filosofii," 11–16.
23. Khomyakov, *Polnoie sobranie sochinenii*, 282.
24. Florovsky, *Puti russkogo bogoslovia*, 350.

from sin is given by God through Jesus Christ, who unites himself with those who don't reject him, and who seek the truth, which is in the church. Khomyakov wrote,

> The unity of the church is necessary following from the unity of God, since the church is not the multitude of persons in their separate individuality, but the unity of God's grace, living in the multitude of rational creatures, submitting themselves to grace. Grace is also given to the disobedient, refusing to use it (burying their talents), but they are not in the church. The unity of the church is not imaginary or allegorical, but true and substantial, such as the unity of many members in a living body... The church visible or earthly lives in perfect fellowship and unity with all the body of the church, whose head is Christ. She has Christ in herself and the grace of the Holy Spirit...[25]

Sobornost is a principle, which connects individual humans into a body, or *Sobor*. It expresses the idea of unity in plurality, which is more than unity created by common interests or enforced from the outside. The whole that appears as a result of such unity is more than a sum total of the individuals who combine to make this whole. Such unity is a result of the shared spirituality, which is based on love, and it is the church that makes such unity possible.[26] This unity is an unavoidable part of Christian faith. Florovsky argues that there are no solitary Christians, for Christianity implies a life "within the church,"[27] since outside of it, one can neither grasp the meaning of the Scripture nor perceive the works of God. Yet it becomes possible in the church, because God's Spirit and God's grace is present there.[28]

Sobornost implies that the importance of the church cannot be stressed enough, since outside of the church there is neither salvation nor space for reading or interpreting the Scripture. Hence, as Khomyakov writes, no critique of the church is even possible,

> But wisdom, which lives in you, is not given to you as a person, but to you as a member of the Church. It is also given in part, without fully destroying your personal lies. Yet the Church has the fullness of wisdom without a trace of lie. For this reason do

---

25. Khomyakov, "Opit Katechezicheskogo Izlozheniia Ucheniia," 3.
26. Florenskii, "Poniatiie tserkvi v sviaschennom pisanii," 81–82.
27. Florovsky, "Dukhovnie Razmishleniia," para. 5.
28. Khomyakov, "Opit Katechezicheskogo Izlozheniia Ucheniia," 7.

not judge the Church, but obey her, so that your wisdom is not taken away from you . . . [29]

Consequently, individual convictions are dismissed as irrelevant, since faith is not something personal or private, but a result of corporate experience—it is about being united to Christ.[30] Popov argues that one of the negative aspects of sobornost is its presupposition of "complete dilution of individuality inside the sacred congregation."[31] Dealing with the theme of biblical interpretation in Russian Baptist churches, he offers a helpful insight into what sobornost means for preaching and biblical interpretation,

> In preaching, sobornost implies the equality or even the identity of preachers and parishioners. It supposes that preachers are just the mouth of the congregation. In the opinion of Orthodox Christians, a priest's words cannot come into contradiction with the common spirit of the congregation. That is why the proclamations of the preachers, as a rule, are impersonal. For example, they use the pronoun "we" instead of "I." Sobornost implies also an uncritical reception of preaching. The authority of leaders stands above any doctrine or ethical norm. Criticism of the clergy in Orthodoxy is one of the gravest sins.[32]

Let me offer a brief summary of the argument up to this point. According to Orthodox theologians, sobornost cannot be properly rationally explained and understood. It has to be experienced by being part of the church through the mystical unity with Christ, since sobornost is not a human characteristic, but a quality of God. Thus at the heart of the doctrine of sobornost is a teaching about the church being seen as the mystical and invisible body of Christ. Such understanding highlights the nature of the sacraments, understood as acts which are exclusively within the church and for the church. Since the church is a reality which is beyond reason, sacraments do not require rational understanding.[33] Although preaching is not present in the traditionally accepted list of sacraments,[34] some Orthodox theologians perceive it as sacramental in character, particularly through the

29. Ibid., 8.
30. Florovsky, *Puti russkogo bogoslovia*, 351.
31. Popov, "Evangelical Christians-Baptists," 125.
32. Ibid., 125.
33. Khorunjii, *Posle pereriva*, 6. See also Khomyakov, *Polnoie sobranie sochinenii*, 115.
34. Although there is no list of sacraments that is universally recognized by all Orthodox churches, the generally accepted ones are Baptism, Chrismation, Eucharist, Confession, Marriage, Holy Orders, and Anointing of the Sick.

sacrament of Holy Orders or priesthood.[35] Hence, God continues to work through the act of preaching regardless of its rhetorical value—God's work is a mystery, which happens through the act itself.

Preaching in the Russian Orthodox Church

The subject of preaching in the Russian Orthodox Church has attracted a lot of attention from secular and religious authors, covering a wide spectrum of aspects from the overview of its development through history to the analysis of preaching as a genre of public speech. Since it is neither possible nor necessary to address all those issues here, I will concentrate on a particular period in the development of preaching—the late nineteenth and early twentieth centuries—to gain an insight into the context in which the first Russian baptistic communities were being shaped.

There were two main approaches to preaching in the Orthodox Church. The rhetorical approach emphasized practical methods of conviction and persuasion. It was developed at the end of the seventeenth century by Archimandrit Ioannikii Gol'atovskii and later by Bishop Fiofan Prokopovich.[36] The followers of this homiletical school believed teaching people the Christian faith and persuading them to change their lives can be done through rhetorical devices and convincing argumentation.[37]

In 1846, professor Amphiteatrov from Kiev Theological Seminary published an extensive work on homiletics, where he rejected the idea that preaching was a form of rhetoric. Rather, the main task of homiletics was to define the conditions that would allow the appearance of the true sermon, thus shifting the focus from the sermon to the "soul of the preacher."[38] In this approach, preaching is understood as embodiment of God's energy given to the preacher, who then transmits it to the listeners. Thus, preaching is, first of all, the work of God, the result of God's grace. The gift of preaching is given through priesthood.[39]

Such an approach rejects rhetoric, since God's word does not need human constructs to be made more convincing.[40] This approach, also known as anti-rhetorical or charismatic, was prevalent in the Orthodox Church in

35. *Nastol'naia kniga*, 9.
36. Ibid., 7–8.
37. Prokhvatilova, *Pravoslavnaia propoved i molitva*, 127.
38. *Nastol'naia kniga*, 8.
39. Ibid., 9.
40. Prokhvatilova, *Pravoslavnaia propoved i molitva*, 127.

the second half of the nineteenth and the beginning of the twentieth century. Although there were several attempts to combine the two approaches, the task is still viewed as incomplete and requiring further work.[41]

The Priest's Handbook offers the following interpretation of charismatic preaching:

> Apostolic preaching was not just continuation of preaching of the Lord Jesus Christ. It was the very word of the Savior proclaimed through the disciples. The center of the apostles' preaching was the testimony of the Truth, embodied in the Crucified Christ (1 Cor 2:3), Resurrected and Redeeming the world . . . Preaching of the apostles became a special ministry, "the ministry of the word" (Acts 6:4; Eph 3:7) for which the Lord Jesus Christ gave the apostles the Grace of the Holy Spirit and His co-presence (Acts 1:8; Matt 28:20, and others). That is why apostolic preaching is "not in convincing words of human wisdom, but in the appearance of the Spirit and power" (1 Cor 2:4). This is the foundation of its full success.[42]

The preaching of the apostles is seen as an ideal which nevertheless is impossible to achieve since no one can attain the knowledge of the apostles and their closeness to God. This brings a problem of proclaiming one's views and not God's word. The solution is seen as twofold. First is the need for the preacher to reject his own will in everything, allowing the truth to act in and through his life. The second is the role of the church and its teaching, which serves as a guardian of the sound teaching and protects preaching from heresies.[43]

Olga Prokhvatilova[44] defines several main characteristic features of preaching. Firstly, preaching is God-inspired, "since the word is self-expressed through preaching." This mystical process of incarnation of the word into a human language can allow space for rhetoric. Yet the weakness and inadequacy of human words cannot thwart God's purposes, which will be achieved regardless of the quality of the presentation—after all, God is at work in preaching. Secondly, it is the coexistence of the two worlds, the divine and human. The Creator reveals himself through the proclaimed word to human beings. Thirdly, preaching brings salvation by facilitating

---

41. *Nastol'naia kniga*, 9.

42. Ibid., 12.

43. Ibid., 13.

44. Dr. Olga Prokhvatilova is a professor of Volgograd State University. She is one of the leading specialists in the area of Russian Orthodox preaching.

contact between people and the truth, which is Christ and his word. Such an encounter results in listeners gaining greater knowledge about God, but also brings moral and spiritual growth, causing repentance and purification. Finally, preaching is an expression of sobornost, as it is directed at a gathering of individual Christians who, whilst maintaining their individuality, are united as listeners of the word. The power of spiritual unity with other believers gathered in the temple and with Christ enables the listeners to perceive and experience the truth during the sermon.[45]

The strong conviction that Christ himself is present in preaching, which is his words being proclaimed, bears implications for the preacher's preparation. The preacher must come into the worship having spent time in repentance and prayer, which enables him to fight sin and to observe God through prayerful reflection. This, and regular participation in the liturgical life of the church, allows God's gracious powers to work in the preacher's mind, helping him to understand the truth.[46] This is a required preparation for a sermon. The content of a message therefore is less important—the right heart is the key. Such an approach is well illustrated with the following words about the preaching of Metropolitan Filaret,

> When people listened to him, they listened very intensely. Yet they could not understand the words of the preacher, and only heard the sound of his voice and felt the look of his eyes. It was enough to feed their spirit with the spirit of the great elder. This is the power of the spirit-led preaching. In it the spirit of the preacher immediately works on the listener's spirit.[47]

Henceforth, it is argued that preaching must be extemporaneous, allowing the Spirit to speak. An improvised sermon, proclaimed in the power of the Spirit is capable of bringing the word of God to the people, allowing them to participate in the act of God's revelation. Extemporaneous preaching is considered superior to the message prepared in advance, since "all the work of transmitting the spiritual riches of the preacher into the living word happens in the temple, during the preaching event."[48]

Preaching is seen as "a culmination of the Divine Liturgy,"[49] which is directed outwardly. The role of proclamation is to carry saving truth to the

---

45. Prokhvatilova, *Pravoslavnaia propoved i molitva*, 145–47.
46. *Nastol'naia kniga*, 14.
47. Vetelev, *Istoriia propovednichestva russkoi pravoslavnoi tserkvi*, 84.
48. *Nastol'naia kniga*, 5, 24.
49. Ibid., 15.

hearts of the worshipers. Preaching has such an important place that some Orthodox theologians conclude that preaching by itself is a gift of grace, which priests receive at ordination. Thus, preaching differs from other genres of public speaking. Unlike rhetoric directed at the minds of the listeners (not their hearts), preaching reflects "the experiencing of God's Truth in the soul of the preacher (at that very moment!)."[50]

Orthodox understanding and practice of preaching differs substantially from the paradigm offered in the majority of preaching textbooks written by homilists from baptistic or the wider Protestant tradition. In the Orthodox Church, preaching is seen as a transmission not only of God's words, but also as a channel of God's saving grace. Therefore, even when the message does not contain a coherent structure, theological depth, or any relevance for the listeners, it can still be seen as successful. If the preacher's spiritual condition is right, God will deliver the necessary meaning into the hearts, minds, and lives of the listeners.

Conclusion

The complex, multi-origin nature of the birth and development of the baptistic movement in the Russian Empire meant the absence of a coherent theological framework within which these communities appeared. Considering the dominant Orthodox theological environment and the extent to which Orthodox convictions and practices penetrated every sphere of Russian culture, it would be wrong to assume that baptistic groups were capable of separating themselves from it. Thus, unlike certain visible practices such as veneration of icons (which was an easy target for baptistic criticism), more complex theological convictions underlying views on salvation, holiness, the role of the church, and many others were absorbed by baptistic Christians as their own. Similarly, the anti-rhetorical or charismatic preaching, which dominated Orthodox pulpits at a time when the first baptistic groups appeared on the religious stage of the Russian Empire, have left a major imprint on their understanding and practice of preaching.

50. Ibid., 15.

3

Development of Russian Baptistic Preaching

Introduction

ANY STUDY OF THE development of Russian baptistic[1] preaching is bound to face difficulties. Firstly, it is nearly impossible to rely on primary sources—the texts of the sermons. Russian society has always been predominantly an oral culture; therefore, writing manuscripts has never been customary for preachers. Moreover, the established Orthodox tradition of charismatic preaching, with its emphasis on the importance of extemporaneous preaching without the use of the written manuscript, has made a significant impact on baptistic groups. Finally, baptistic believers, like any dissenters from the Orthodox Church, were experiencing constant persecution both under the tsarist government and the communistic regime, which was responsible for the destruction of those documents that were collected in the archives of various local churches and individuals.

Nevertheless, there are a number of sources that can be used for such study. Firstly, a variety of resources originated from baptistic groups that include publications in their magazines and newspapers from the beginning of the twentieth century; a number of books written in the second half of the twentieth century and some articles in the *BV*, as well as books, articles, and dissertations that appeared in recent years, covering various

---

1. The historical overview in this chapter focuses on Stundist communities, churches of Evangelical Christians, as well as communities of RUECB. Therefore I refer to all these ecclesial groups as "baptistic," using a lowercase "b."

areas of Russian Baptist hermeneutics and ecclesiology. Another category is comprised of publications by Orthodox authors, including critical, sometimes hostile works produced particularly during the late nineteenth and early twentieth centuries. Several secular books appeared during the communistic period as part of state battle with religious faith. Some of them lack any academic value, being examples of overt atheistic propaganda. Yet a number of these publications contain serious and fairly objective observations and reflections on baptistic life and worship. I will refer to these sources later in this chapter.

Throughout all the stages of their history, Russian baptistic churches had to deal with the process of contextualization of their message and practices. During the formative years, from the appearance of the first known baptistic groups (approx. in 1862), they were learning to cope with the Bible instead of the tradition as the main source for their life and faith. Emphasis on personal ethics and highly critical views of the Orthodox clergy was important to justify the dissent. The second period begins with the Edict of Religious Toleration and the Revolution of 1905, which allowed Russian citizens to leave the Orthodox Church. The greater religious freedom, changes in the political sphere, and aspirations for more democratic re-shaping of the state brought forward new challenges for the church, such as openness to the newcomers, training of missionaries and pastors, thus resulting in a more pragmatic, professional approach to preaching and ministerial formation. Finally, it raised questions of theological coherence in a context of a growing number of self-taught and home-grown teachers and evangelists.

The law from April 8, 1929 "About Religious Organizations" allowed free preaching only to the newly established religion—atheism. Thus it marks the beginning of the third period—the Communistic oppression, which covers a wide epoch from the beginning of persecutions until the end of the dark era during Mikhail Gorbachov's perestroika (1989). Ongoing severe persecution from the communistic regime, and the impossibility to either develop theological training or even receive advanced secular education for the believers—all of that resulted in the decrease of the value of education in the eyes of both church leaders and ordinary Christians. Unsurprisingly, one of the outcomes of that epoch can be seen in over-spiritualization of preaching as a practice, with spirituality of the preacher, his piety and faithfulness to the calling becoming more important than the message he was proclaiming.

Development of Russian Baptistic Preaching

A new period of openness and freedom (fourth period, from 1989 to modern time[2]), which neither church nor society has ever experienced, mounted the biggest challenge to the church—how to make its message relevant not only to the new-comers, but also to its long-standing members. This highlights the growing need of identifying the core convictions, the constants of the baptistic identity and learning to preserve those constants, thus freeing the church from the constraints of less significant elements of its life and worship, which therefore, could be dropped without fear of compromising its identity.

Formative Years

The first thirty-five years of the baptistic movement in Russia is a significant period, which is almost impossible to cover in a short overview. As it has been shown through my narrative up to this point, there was a variety of situations where churches appeared and grew: small peasant communities in Ukrainian villages, Baptist churches in Tiflis (present-day Tbilisi, Georgia), and the meetings in the palaces of aristocracy in St. Petersburg. Multitudes of people were the driving force behind the spread and growth of the movement. Michail Ratushnii, Ivan Ryaboshapka, Vasilii Pashkov, Nikita Voronin, Ivan Kargel[3], Ivan Prokhanov[4], and others mentioned in this book are just a few amongst countless evangelists, preachers, and teachers. Baptists

---

2. It might be possible to argue that the so-called *Yarovaya Law* (a package of amendments to Russian Federal Law on fighting terrorism, Number 374-F3 from July 6, 2016) marks the beginning of a new era in the church-state relationships in Russia, with severe restrictions of missionary and other religious activities in the country.

3. Ivan (Johann) Kargel was one of the most influential leaders of the Russian baptistic movement. Born to a family of German colonists in Georgia, Kargel became an Evangelical Christian through Pashkov, and later became a pastor of the St. Petersburg congregation of Evangelical Christians. As noted by Nichols, Kargel's writings "helped to shape the Russian evangelical movement and Russian Baptist expressions of evangelical spirituality." (*Development of Russian Evangelical Spirituality*, 1)

4. Ivan Prokhanov, one of the key leaders of the Evangelical Christians in Russia, was born to a Molokan family in Vladikavkaz (North Caucasus), and joined a Baptist church in 1887. In the following years he studied theology in various schools in England, Germany, and France. After his return to Russia in 1898, he became actively involved in various ministries of Evangelical Christians. He became a leader of the movement, and is known for his educational programs, publishing activities, and a grand vision for the baptistic believers to bring about the transformation of Russia.

accomplished a fascinating journey developing from small Bible study groups to large organizations consisting of thousands of churches.

Unfortunately, despite all the progress, Baptists produced little written material on their theology and almost nothing on their practices (and particularly practices of worship). There were of course more pressing matters for them, such as survival in the hostile environment of tsarist Russia, developing some denominational structures, and, most importantly, advancing their missionary endeavors. Nonetheless, books, articles, and reports written by Orthodox scholars, reporters, and even police create a significant pool of information about baptistic worship practices at the end of the nineteenth century. Whilst some of this information has little historical value, apart from being another indicator of hostility that the established church had towards nonconformity, some offer a genuine attempt to study a new, and at times controversial, phenomenon on the Russian religious scene.

Priest Arsenii Rozhdestvenskii provides a number of descriptions of Stundist worship practices, focusing on several major areas, such as religious songs, preaching, and prayer.[5] He describes it as follows:

> Having gathered at someone's home, Stundists sit at the benches, and one of them is chairing the gathering. This person sits at a table facing the rest of the congregation. He opens the New Testament or the Bible and interprets every verse. After the reading of the New Testament or the Bible there are various contemplations, often polemical in nature. Then they open another book . . . One person reads the first verse of some spiritual song, if the meaning of anything is unclear, it is explained first, than the rest of the congregation sing the verse altogether. Then they sing another verse, and another. Then they kneel and one of the Stundists offers a passionate extemporaneous prayer, often with tears in his eyes.[6]

Rozhdestvenskii also refers to an account from the newspaper *Pravda (Truth)* from 1878, which provides the following description of a Stundist preaching,

> A sermon consisted of the preacher's reading and offering his explanation of the parable about 10 virgins. The sermon was ended

---

5. Rozhdestvenskii, *Yuzhno-russkii stundism*, 243.
6. Ibid., 251.

with an invitation to the brothers to offer another interpretation, if anyone had one. That was followed by a prayer.[7]

Margaritov also addresses the subject of preaching among Stundists and Evangelical Christians, making an interesting observation—once the preacher finished his sermon, other people, both men and women, were allowed to share their thoughts on the subject, even if they disagreed with the main speaker.[8]

Such a description highlights the centrality of oral biblical interpretation for the worship of early Russian baptists. Kushnev, an Orthodox priest from Orel, whilst being critical of any dissenters from the orthodoxy, accusing them of betrayal not only of their faith but also of the country, notes that although Stundists did not have a theological system their reading of the Scripture (in most cases without guidance from trained theologians) produced stunning results in their moral living.[9] With limited theological training, *Chitai kak napisano* ("Read as it is written") was their main hermeneutical principle; the Bible was read as a book written directly for them. Stundists insisted that the Bible, being the word of God contained everything that was needed for salvation. Every Christian was given God's grace that enabled them to read and understand the Scripture.[10] Furthermore, the ministry of the word was seen as a task of every believer rather than a chosen few as in the Orthodox Church. Hence, a lot of Stundist and Baptist preaching contained overt criticism of the Orthodox Church, its worship practices, and priests, whose behavior was seen as contradictory to the teaching of Christ.[11]

Several points highlighted by Rozhdestvenskii were to be expected at the beginning of a new movement with passion for reformation of the established church. The discovery of the biblical message and particularly its ethical teaching, as well as dissatisfaction with the existing order of social and ecclesial life, caused dissent. Prosecution by the police, fueled by the clergy, widened the split. Final separation was justified by underlining a loss by the Orthodox Church of the true and narrow way. As noted by Leskov, "Everything from start to finish boiled down to one point: the Russian

---

7. Ibid., 251.
8. Margaritov, *Istoriia russkikh misticheskikh i ratsionalisticheskikh sect*, 166, 211.
9. Kushnev, *Nemetskie very*, 11.
10. Ibid., 25.
11. Rozhdestvenskii, *Yuzhno-russkii stundism*, 111–66.

Church was formalistic and lifeless, and they had 'taken against it.'"[12] Thus came the rejection of the tradition (the writings of the Holy Fathers, and liturgical worship), perceived as deviation from the clear biblical message. Instead, Baptists offered a focus on repentance and holy living,[13] which quickly became the marks of the new movement.

A wave of evangelical groups needed some coherence in teaching and practice. In April 1884, Vasilii Pashkov tried to organize a conference which was supposed to bring together representatives from the baptistic communities from all across the Russian Empire (the police had forcefully stopped the meetings). The agenda included questions on the Lord's Supper, baptism, and ordination. As Andrey Puzynin noted, "Pashkov believed that when the Bible is read in a spirit of mutual love, then the community of people from various backgrounds will inevitably come to a common understanding of Scripture on all the questions."[14]

Despite the opposition of the authorities, at the end of the same month another meeting was held in Novo-Vasilievka. This meeting is identified by many historians as a starting point in the history of the Russian Baptist Union.[15] The letter written by Ivan Kargel to Pashkov provides a summary of that meeting, highlighting biblical interpretation and application as the burning issues. Practical questions related to marriage and divorce, ordination, communion, and spiritual gifts were directly linked to the teaching of the Bible. The concluding remarks of this letter are of extreme importance. It was decided that, concerning decisions on various theological issues, "there may exist difference of opinion. It is seen appropriate to seek unani-

---

12. Leskov, *Schism in High Society*, 100–1.

13. Themes of repentance, prayer, and holy living were not an exclusively baptistic concept. Repentance was of extreme importance in the Orthodox tradition, whilst tears during repentance were seen as confirmation of its integrity. Moreover, a moral way of life was often seen as more important for salvation than "sacramental sanctification." (Fedotov, *Russian Religious Mind*, 382–89). Another important source of convictions that influenced the baptistic movement were Molokans, an indigenous evangelical movement that appeared in the late eighteenth century. Molokans rejected the hierarchy within the church, believing that every member of the congregation had a right to read and interpret the Bible both in their private life and in corporate worship (Brandenburg, *Meek and the Mighty*, 62). Thousands of Molokans eventually joined baptistic churches.

14. This understanding eventually changed, as Pashkov came to the conclusion that unity did not exclude diversity of interpretation. (Puzynin, "Tradition of the Gospel Christians," 91)

15. At this stage, growing links to European Baptists played an important role in shaping the structure of the congregations, and in developing their common theological stance.

mous acceptance of decisions, but congregations are to be given the right to decide as they see fit to do before God."[16]

I have already touched upon the practices of reading the Bible among the Stundists and addressed a number of important Orthodox concepts that had a significant impact on the way Baptists in Russia understood and practiced their faith. Before moving on to the next period in their history, it would be helpful to focus on some of the most significant influences that contributed to the shaping of convictions related to biblical interpretation among Baptists and Evangelical Christians.

Baptists were the only group within the Russian baptistic movement that began as a different denomination.[17] Its starting point is generally accepted to be the baptism of a Molokan leader, Nikita Voronin, on August 20, 1867 (despite the fact that some Stundist groups practiced baptism by immersion a few years prior to that), in Tiflis.[18] Voronin was baptized by a German Baptist, Martin Kalweit, who was connected to Johann Gerhard Oncken. Three years later, Voronin was already a presbyter of a church of seventy-eight baptized members.[19] In 1875 the church sent Vasilii Pavlov[20] to Hamburg to study at the Baptist Seminary, which was organized by Oncken.[21]

The congregation in Tiflis accepted the Hamburg confession of faith, and following a German Baptist lead developed a number of rules concerning worship practices and church life. Baptism by immersion and strict moral living were prerequisites for a church membership and participation in the Lord's Supper.[22] Although theologically Russian Baptists were less diverse than Stundists or Evangelical Christians, having appropriated a number of doctrines and practices from German Baptists, they did not

16. Klippenste, "Russian Evangelicalism Revisited," 43–46.

17. Brandenburg, *Meek and the Mighty*, xii.

18. Wardin, "Penetration of Baptists," 45.

19. Karev, "Russkoie evangelsko-baptistskoie dvizheniie," 93, 110.

20. Vasilii Pavlov was born in 1854 to a Molokan family; he joined a Baptist church in Tiflis in 1871. In 1876, he completed a course at the Baptist seminary in Hamburg. Having being ordained for Christian ministry by Oncken, he became a pastor of a church in 1880. Pavlov played an important role in the formation of the Russian Baptist union. He is also known for his missionary efforts, educational work, and publishing activities, including the translation of numerous sermons and theological works written by English and German theologians (See Popov, *Stopi blagovestnika*).

21. Savinskii, *Istoriia evangelskikh khristian-baptistov*, 135.

22. In this, and a number of other church practices, Baptists differed from both Stundists and Evangelical Christians (Kushnev, *Nemetskiie very*, 134–37).

develop any rigid theological system. There always existed a lot of flexibility in interpreting the Scripture.[23]

Puzynin in his analysis of Lord Radstock's biblical interpretation and theological views, argued that the roots of the hermeneutical approach, practiced by Pashkovites, should be placed in Anglo-American evangelicalism. He points to the fact that Radstock for a number of years belonged to the Brethren movement, and thus was coming with certain theological presuppositions to the Scripture. Henceforth, despite his insistence that he was merely reading the Bible, Radstock was clearly bringing an alternative theological and hermeneutical tradition to that of the Orthodox Church:

> The theological hermeneutics of Radstock was of a typological, Christocentric, literalist, pneumatic and experiential nature typical of the hermeneutics of the emerging holiness movement. . . Biblical texts were read through the grid of preconceived theological frameworks in order to achieve two major goals: the conversion of nominal Christians, and the edification of born-again Christians. In the process of producing the desired meaning, Radstock would not be constrained by literary or historical contexts. Typological interpretation was used with both Old and New Testament texts. Biblical personages were used as types either of the contemporary audience or of the transcendent Christ.[24]

Radstock believed that reading the Bible was sufficient to enable a Christian to understand and follow the way of Christ. As noted by Nicolay Leskov, Radstock's success among St. Petersburg's nobility was not due to his eloquence or exquisite manners. Rather, it was his simple faith and the immediacy in his relationship to God that made people interested in his message.[25]

In the life and teaching of Colonel Pashkov, who was converted through Radstock's preaching, one can see a more radical split from the Orthodox Church than that of the Stundists. From being a nominal Christian, he turned into a passionate supporter of the new Christian movement, known for its grand-scale charity and educational projects inspired by biblical teaching. Pashkov viewed his conversion and subsequent transformation as a direct work of Christ. He believed that after the conversion,

---

23. Russian Baptist churches hold diverse views on salvation and predestination, which is considered acceptable by the leadership of the Union (Podberezskii, "O kalvinizme, kharismatii, voiennoi sluzhbe," 35).

24. Puzynin, "Tradition of the Gospel Christians," 51.

25. Leskov, *Schism in High Society,* 112–14, 196–97.

the Holy Spirit continued to work in the life of a Christian, helping them to understand the biblical narrative. Thus, he rejected the teaching of the Orthodox Church about the important role of the tradition, instead insisting on the prayerful reading of the Bible to allow the Holy Spirit to reveal its true meaning.[25]

Puzynin argues that Radstock, and later Pashkov, were bringing western evangelical paradigms into the Russian Empire. He shows similarities of their teaching to Brethren views on the Bible, and highlights the gradual deviation of Pashkovites from the Orthodox Church. One of the most important things that Pashkov (and Evangelical Christians as a whole) learned from Radstock was a hermeneutical tool of literal and typological reading of the Scripture. As Princess Lieven wrote, Lord Radstock was to be thanked for opening the richness and depth of the Bible to the Evangelical Christians, which made them strongly rooted in the Scripture, thus enabling them to stand firm during the persecutions.[27]

However, Puzynin notes, "Pashkov was obviously unaware of the theological and philosophical filter he had inherited from Radstock with regard to the interpretation of the Bible."[28] Hence, Pashkov's theological stance was not grounded in any theological system. Rather, it was characterized by the lack of doctrinal knowledge (either Protestant or Orthodox) and heavy reliance on direct quotations from the New Testament. Theologically, Pashkov shared many convictions with Russian Baptists and Stundists, all of whom did not have any other common ground, but a worldview shaped by the Orthodox spirituality and literal reading and application of the Scripture to their life and faith.

The initial formative years of the Russian baptistic movement show the fascinating complexity of factors that have contributed to the development of the character of contemporary Baptists in Russia. The movement had indigenous roots (Molokans and some Stundist groups), yet was influenced by both British (Pashkovites) and German (Baptists) Christians. It started in different geographical areas (St. Petersburg, Odessa, and Tiflis are now located in three different countries). It had dissimilar social composition (from wealthy aristocrats in the North to poor peasants in the South). There was no uniformity even in its denominational stance; Baptists had clear denominational affiliation, whilst many Pashkovites did not want to

26. Puzynin, "Tradition of the Gospel Christians," 72–97.
27. Lieven, *Dukhovnoie probuzdeniie v Rossii*, 32.
28. Puzynin, "Tradition of the Gospel Christians," 74.

break away from the Orthodox Church even after their leaders were exiled from the country. Despite the differences, these groups were similar in their theology and ecclesiology. All of them were characterized by the emphasis they placed on the importance of individual and communal Bible study. Every Christian had a right to interpret the Holy Scriptures; everyone had a duty to share God's message with others.

Freedom to interpret God's word without the constraints of a particular dogmatic theology played an important role in the quick spread of the baptistic movement. Simple proclamation of biblical truth of salvation interpreted through the lenses of the Orthodox understanding of holy living rang true to the hearts of listeners. The message they heard was not a foreign teaching, but an embodiment of the gospel truth, already deeply rooted in their society. A lack of style or clarity in the sermons that were proclaimed by mostly self-taught preachers was not a distraction either—it wasn't much different from the sermons in the Orthodox churches with their heavy emphasis on God's mysterious work in the act of proclamation, regardless of the level of listeners' comprehension of the message.

Big Dreams and Dashed Hopes: 1905–1929

Prior to 1905, Russian law drew a sharp difference between ethnic Russians and non-Russians when it came to questions of religious practice. For example, those Germans who lived in the Russian Empire could belong to Lutheran, Mennonite, and Catholic congregations. Ethnic Russians had to be Orthodox. Only the Russian Orthodox Church was allowed to proselytize among the citizens of the Empire. Conversion to any other faith was a criminal offense.[29] Nonetheless, Baptists and Evangelical Christians were extremely active in spreading their beliefs. The fact that their preaching was supported by their transformed life made it compelling for others.[30] They were so successful in their missionary work that, as Ivan Kushnev noted, by 1916 there was not a village in Russia that did not encounter baptistic witness.[31] Different sources vary in the evaluation of the numerical growth

---

29. Waldron, "Religious Toleration," 103–5.

30. Coleman offers another insight into the fast spread of the Baptist movement in Russia, arguing that Baptists were giving their members a sense of belonging to a new society, escaping social unrest and economic struggles (*Russian Baptists and Spiritual Revolution*, 4).

31. Kushnev, *Nemetskiie very*, 3.

of the baptistic movement, ranging from around 20,000, to 100,000 members before 1905. By 1914, the most conservative estimation is over 50,000 members, whilst others speak about 300,000 or even higher numbers.[32]

Whichever system of counting is employed, it is clear that after 1905, in a relatively short period, the number of baptistic believers doubled or even tripled. Such rapid growth became possible partly due to a new law from April 17, 1905, "On the Strengthening of Religious Toleration." Its implications for all non-Orthodox believers were so great that some considered this law of equal importance to the revolutionary liberation of the serfs by Alexander II.[33] As a result of this legislation, baptistic churches received the right to be officially registered and carry out religious practices without fear of persecution, even though the Orthodox Church remained an established church and preserved its exclusive right to proselytize.[34]

Baptists could not predict how long such freedom would last, thus they channeled their energy into outreach—sending missionaries and planting new churches and Bible-reading groups. Some of them, like Kargel or Prokhanov, became important leaders of the movement, whose heritage is difficult to overestimate. At the same time, there were countless others who went to the distant corners of the Empire driven by their enthusiasm and passion for God's kingdom. They were not taught or sent by any specific congregation. Their only tools were the Bible and preaching. There are even accounts of people turned into preachers after visiting one evangelistic meeting, undergoing conversion, and deciding to commit their life to Christ. Such people did not even have Bibles, and their Christian experience was limited to one or two sermons that had brought them to conversion.

V. V. Ivanov, a pastor from Baku, wrote about this period,

> Armed with the truth of God, (the Baptists) boldly enter into an unequal battle with errors of all sorts and expand their spiritual territory with great success . . . Since 1905 an era has begun in the history of the Baptists that can be called the era of open storm.[35]

The errors were to be expected with Baptists' diverse cultural, theological, and doctrinal backgrounds. Prior to 1905, baptistic communities

---

32. Savinskii, *Istoriia evangelskikh khristian-baptistov*, 262; Sawatsky, *Soviet Evangelicals Since World War II*, 23.

33. Latimer, *Dr. Brazdek and His Apostolic*, 42.

34. Ellis and Jones, *Other Revolution*, 141.

35. Ivanov, "Polozheniie baptistov," 69, quoted after Coleman, *Russian Baptists and Spiritual Revolution*, 27.

held only a small number of conferences where some organizational and theological issues were addressed, hence individual congregations (and preachers) had ultimate authority in the interpretation and application of the Scripture, which with the numerical growth of the movement resulted in a great "interpretive entropy."[36]

The leadership of the movement adopted a number of strategies to cope with the theological diversity of its members, which started to cause various problems in local churches. I have already mentioned that at the meeting that formed the Baptist Union, a conscious decision to allow difference of opinions was made. Congregations were given the right to decide "as they see fit to do before God." Puzynin points out that whilst there always was "a willingness to drop one's own interpretation in order to protect the spirit of mutual love that reflects Trinitarian unity in diversity," various steps were made to create a certain degree of theological unity.[37] Among them were the use of the Apostolic Creed, conferences[38] where various theological and practical issues related to the church life were discussed, and perhaps the most important one, the educational use of publications.

The Christian Printed Media

In the nineteenth and early twentieth centuries, books, journals, and newspapers played a very important role in Russian society. Education became more accessible for poor people only in the second half of the nineteenth century. Thus, for the majority of Russia's population, published materials were first of all associated with sacred texts of the Orthodox Church. Even though this has changed with the rapid development of printed media, "people preserved a special reverence for printed materials, which were extremely valued and trusted."[39] Alexander Popov points out that the power of printed media was so great that some publications (including such novels as Ivan Turgenyev's *Fathers and Sons* and Nicolaii Chernishevsky's *What*

36. Puzynin, "Tradition of the Gospel Christians," 36.

37. Ibid., 36.

38. Baptists and Evangelical Christians achieved significant results in bringing structural coherence to the movements. Two unions were formed—the Congress of Evangelical Christians-Baptists (1905) (CECB) and the All-Russia Union of Evangelical Christians (1909) (ARUEC). Eventually, every region of the country had a local association of churches that coordinated its missionary activities, publications, and spiritual education (Prokhanov, *V kotle Rossii*, 134–50).

39. Popov, "Evangelical Christians-Baptists," 55.

is to be Done?) triggered the start of several social movements.[40] Hence, an extremely strict governmental control and censorship of this area of public life was to be expected.

The role of books and magazines in the development of the baptistic movement is difficult to overestimate. *Colporteurs* were among the first missionaries, distributing Bibles and other spiritual literature, as well as interpreting it to the most uneducated people.[41] Pashkov's Society for the Encouragement of Spiritual and Moral Reading (opened in 1874) has published a large amount of Christian literature, including the works of John Bunyan, collections of Charles Spurgeon's sermons, and various hymns, among other works.[42]

As early as 1889, Prokhanov started Russia's first evangelical periodical *Beseda (A Talk)*.[43] Although it was not possible to receive permission from the authorities for such a publication, it was decided to produce the journal, which was sent all across Russia. Prokhanov wrote,

> The joy from the first copies that reached our brothers and sisters was great. We did not even expect such great feedback . . . These copies of *Beseda* contained spiritual support, encouragements, and we were told again and again that when reading these small pages, brothers received great satisfaction among all kinds of trials, received inner peace and joy into their hearts.[44]

The journal became a model for all the subsequent publications of Evangelical Christians and Baptists.[45]

After 1905, evangelicals received a unique opportunity to legally publish their own newspapers and journals. Prokhanov applied to the government for permission to start this work almost immediately after the appearance of the legislation allowing religious freedom. The first issue

---

40. Ibid., 55.

41. Zacek, "Russian Bible Society," 411–37.

42. Corrado, "Gospel in Society," 52–70. For a list of evangelical books and authors published at the beginning of the twentieth century see Kuznetsova, "Early Russian Evangelicals," 237–39.

43. *Russkii Rabochii (Russian Worker)* was the first magazine published by Russia's evangelicals in 1875. It wasn't a denominational Christian magazine, containing neither materials for Bible study nor sermons. The journal's main thrust was to offer moral guidance to working-class people (Heier, *Religious Schism*, 72).

44. Prokhanov, *V kotle Rossii*, 69–70.

45. Popov, "Evangelical Christians-Baptists," 55.

of *Khristianin* (*The Christian*) saw the light on January 1, 1906.[46] It was published until the end of 1928, when it was closed by Soviet atheistic authorities. Prokhanov formulated three main principles for the periodical. First, to open the essence of Christianity to Russian people, and to show them Christ and his eternal salvation. Second, to encourage evangelism and the building of Russia's evangelical church, aiming at leading people towards reformation of their spiritual being. And finally, to bring unity to all branches of living Christianity in Russia.[47] Puzynin argues that

> These periodicals[48] were the chief means of creating the movement's identity and shaping its theology . . . It allowed all kinds of Christians to share their testimonies, thoughts, and impressions. The key feature of the periodicals of this period was their tendency toward polyphony. Similar to contemporary Internet forums, where everyone can leave a message, the periodicals sometimes contained contradictory viewpoints.[49]

Khristianin contained devotional articles, poems, hymns, sermons of prominent preachers, Bible study material, articles on the history of the church, and stories for children. An important part of the journal were sections on evangelical work in Russia and abroad, thus establishing a link between scattered and oppressed Russian evangelicals with stronger movements around the world. The content of the journal had changed significantly over time. Its first issues contained mostly translated articles and sermons from English and American sources, as well as articles on Christian basics such as "Why do you live?," "Freedom in Christ," "How to pray," "The Holy Spirit," "How to live a happy life," "The outpouring of the Holy Spirit," and "How to have a correct perspective on things." The later issues contain theological materials suitable for more mature Christians, including Kargel's commentaries on various books of the Bible, theological essays by Nicolaii Kazakov, and others. Many issues of the journal featured

---

46. According to Puzynin, *Khristianin* took the same name and structure as the British non-denominational revivalist newspaper *The Christian* ("Tradition of the Gospel Christians," 136–37).

47. Prokhanov, *V kotle Rossii*, 135–36.

48. Apart from *Khristianin*, Evangelical Christians produced *Bratskii Listok* (*The Brotherly Leaflet*), *Molodoi Vinogradnik* (*Young Vineyard*), and *Utrenniaia Zvezda* (*Morning Star*). For more detailed insight into the goals of these periodicals see Puzynin, "Tradition of the Gospel Christians," 136–38; Coleman, *Russian Baptists and Spiritual Revolution*, 30–34; Kuznetsov, "Nashi evangelskie zhurnaly," 65.

49. Puzynin, "Tradition of the Gospel Christians," 138.

sermon outlines prepared for preachers to use in churches across the country. Such a service had a double aim—it was an important ministry for small congregations, which used the journal as their primary source of teaching material, and at the same time, as a result of such mass preaching, the leadership of the Union could achieve greater theological coherence in otherwise diverse congregations.

Baptist, the journal of the Baptist Union[50] was similar to *Khristianin* in its pattern, use, and purposes. However, it maintained a much clearer denominational stance. The issues of the journal regularly contained articles on Baptist beliefs, the meaning of the term "Baptist," and many others, explaining the difference between Baptists and Orthodox, and between the Baptist Union and other evangelicals. This was different from Prokhanov's *Khristianin*, which appeared as more broadly evangelical and "showed no denominational narrowness."[51]

Christian Education

Publications proved to be a precious tool for baptistic leadership in developing and shaping their congregations. They brought a sense of unity, enabling even the most remote churches to feel that they were part of a greater community of believers across Russia and beyond. Journals offered educational materials on baptistic convictions, church history, and biblical theology, thus partly solving the problem of subjectivism in biblical interpretation. Finally, conversion narratives, which were often featured in these publications, helped to challenge readers' spiritual development and cultivated a call to, and urgency for, evangelistic work.[52] All of the above contributed to a formation of particular denominational identities.

50. The first issue of the journal was published in June 1907. With some breaks the journal was published until 1929, when it was finally closed by the communistic authorities, as part of their war with religion (Sinichkin, "Istoriia zhurnala 'Baptist'").

51. Brandenburg, *Meek and the Mighty*, 134.

52. Coleman argued that "Russian Baptists' conversion stories usually drive home the point that, in the end, neither the religious traditions of their youths nor revolutionary politics could offer them the assurance of salvation that they craved. Instead, Baptist auto-biographers emphasize the role of ordinary believers in shaping the thinking of potential converts and in guiding them toward achieving salvation. In so doing, they paint a picture of an egalitarian, self-educating movement of working people." Thus uneducated people were given an urge to evangelize, reach out to the fallen world of sin (For an extensive analysis of the use of conversion narratives, see Coleman, *Russian Baptists and Spiritual Revolution*, ch. 3).

As I have previously stated, preaching was given special attention in publications. It was assumed that the best way to teach preachers was by providing an example. Thus every issue of *Khristianin* and *Baptist* contained at least one sermon from a famous baptist preacher (Spurgeon, Prokhanov, W. Fetler, Moody, just to name a few). Numerous stories from various Christian churches and situations, both from a Russian context and from Anglo-American Christian culture, were offered and used as important preaching material. Preaching notes and sermon outlines provided another way to help pastors in their ministry. Finally, although irregularly, journals published extended articles on how to preach.

Apart from the recognition of the benefits of using printed media, from the early years of baptistic movement in Russia, its leaders showed appreciation for Christian education. Dei Mazaev, who served as a president of the Russian Baptist Union for over twenty years, at the end of the nineteenth century, indicated the need for developing theological schools. He called people to pray, asking God to send ministers, "clothed in contemporary theological education."[53] It was recognized that society was changing and certain views and practices required modification. Mikhail Timoshenko, one of the Baptist leaders, wrote, "When God's work only started to develop, whoever opened the Gospel were fascinated—everything was new, unknown, thus interesting. Today we live in a different time, hence we've got new requirements."[54] Preparation of people for ministry through formal educational arrangements was seen as a way forward.

One of the first projects initiated by Prokhanov after 1905 was the organization of a six-week study course for young preachers. They were taught biblical interpretation, theology, homiletics, and church history. The unusual features of these courses were nontheological disciplines—grammar, Russian literature, history, and geography.[55] Among the teachers were Kargel, Prokhanov, Pavel Nikolaii, and other Evangelical Christian or Baptist leaders. Despite continuous struggle with the authorities, the permission to open a school was only received in 1913. Nineteen students were enrolled in the first year. Among them were Lithuanians, German Mennonites, Georgians, Ossetians, Belorussians, and Russians.[56] The work of the school was interrupted during World War I, yet it was restarted in

---

53. Nagirniak, "Bibleiskiie kursi baptistov," 107.
54. Timoshenko, "Kafedra," 285.
55. Karetnikova, "U istokov sovremennogo religioznogo obrazovaniia," 68.
56. Prokhanov, *V kotle Rossii*, 164–65.

1922 and operated until 1929. During this period, over 450 people were trained for ministry.[57]

The first Baptist training center operated in Lodz, Poland (at that time part of the Russian Empire). The school was opened by German Baptists and for a long time remained the only Baptist school in Russia. From 1922 to 1924, Pavlov together with Sergei Stephanov led short theology and preaching courses in different areas of the country. After a number of appeals, the authorities allowed the Baptist Union to open a Bible school in Moscow in 1927. However, it only operated for two years, being closed at the beginning of a new wave of atheistic persecutions of the church.[58] On the other side of Russia, in its Far Eastern region, Christian education was first of all connected with such names as Yakov Vince, Robert Fetler, Nikolai Peisti, Eric Olson, and August Lindstedt. All of these people were trained in England, the USA, Germany, Sweden, or Finland.[59] They started a number of educational programs for Baptist missionaries and pastors from 1919 to 1922. The skills related to preaching were given particular attention, since preaching was seen as a key ability, necessary for missionary and pastoral work. Whilst there is no record left regarding the content of the abovementioned programs, the existence of numerous links to various western (particularly American) educational institutions allows one to assume a high degree of borrowing and adapting western materials to the realities of post-revolutionary Russia.[60]

Now I would like to have a closer look at Prokhanov's work, particularly in relation to his homiletical views. Prokhanov played an extremely important role in the baptistic movement in Russia at the beginning of the twentieth century through the leadership position he held with Evangelical Christians, his publishing activity, and his efforts in developing Christian education.[61] In order to understand a trajectory that baptistic preaching was taking, it would be helpful to explore Prokhanov's views on this ministry as

---

57. Popov, "Otechestvenniaia shkola propovedi v tserkvakh," 39.

58. Nagirniak, "Bibleiskiie kursy baptistov," 103–14.

59. Dementiev, *Evangelskoie dvizheniie v Primorie*, 63, 65.

60. Potapova, "Vosproizvodstvo kadrov," 74–92.

61. The Bible courses, which Prokhanov directed in Leningrad (now St. Petersburg) until his emigration from the USSR, were especially important since some of its graduates became teachers at the Bible Correspondent Courses (BCC) of AUCECB—the only Baptist educational program that existed during the Soviet era (Mitskevich, *Istoriia evangelskikh khristian-baptistov*, 405).

they are reflected in a collection of his essays, which later was published as a book called *Short Teaching on Preaching*.

In this collection, Prokhanov explains his passion for developing evangelical education as a holistic alternative to existing religious practices,

> (T)he religious condition of Russian people nowadays is tragic. It is true that people have gilded temples, pompous worship, famous pulpits, from which taught preachers[62] proclaim sermons, created according to all the rules of homiletics—and even censored by the highest spiritual authorities, - yet, alas! All of that does not satisfy people's needs. Why is it so?
>
> To this we can answer: first of all because of the inner state of the preachers and the people; because of the lack of the true faith, and subsequent absence of life and the power of the Spirit in these official sermons. Sermons proclaimed from official pulpits speak about rituals, about philosophy, they are full of polemics with other religions, yet they are silent about the most important thing—about living Christ, as a source of salvation and life . . .
>
> But God did not leave our people without his visitation. He is sending his spiritual bread to the people, which is God's Word, which was hidden from the people for hundreds of years, and yet, which resulted in Russia's Evangelical movement and which has given us new Gospel preaching.[63]

Prokhanov's goal was to bring spiritual renewal and transformation to the whole of Russia (causing a rift from the CECB, which did not perceive such intense involvement with the wider society as a biblically sound pursuit). He viewed preaching as one of the key tools in reaching that grand vision. Hence, a lot of effort was invested in organizing the Bible school, courses, and seminars on biblical interpretation and preaching. His lectures highlighted the importance of studying the discipline of homiletics and applying its insights to the process of preparation and delivery of a sermon. At the same time, he did not discard prevailing highly spiritualized views on preaching, saying that "Desire to study preaching, turned into a science

---

62. This quote requires a clarifying remark. Being a passionate proponent of theological education and homiletics, Prokhanov's sharp critique of "taught preachers" has to be seen in a context of the prevailing Orthodox ecclesial culture and aimed at Orthodox preaching. It was assumed that evangelical preaching was done in the power of the Holy Spirit.

63. Prokhanov, *Kratkoie ucheniie o propovedy*, Introduction.

about preaching, resulted in a deadly formalism . . . Preaching in its highest meaning is the word of God transmitted through the lips of a man."[64]

Prokhanov believed that although the success of preaching depended fully on it conforming to God's will, its content, style of delivery, and the personality of a preacher also played an important role. Therefore, he argued that Christian education was a necessity, pointing at the disciples of Jesus, who had spent over three years with the greatest teacher of all time, dismissing a view that the apostles were uneducated fishermen. At the same time, Prokhanov addresses the problem of scholastic preaching, irrelevant for the church due to the preacher's inability to understand its everyday life. Thus, he believed that seminary training should be linked to the practical ministry.[65] Similarly, without denying the importance of the inspiration from the Holy Spirit in the process of sermon preparation, Prokhanov insisted on the significance of the preacher's contribution to it. Moreover, he criticized the views of the proponents of purely extemporaneous preaching, who believed that the Holy Spirit inspired people only during the event of proclamation itself.[66]

Prokhanov argued that preaching should always preserve the spirit of the teaching of Christ as presented in the New Testament. It must "imitate Christ's preaching,"[57] which means that preachers can only interpret the great truths of Christ and help their listeners to apply them to their lives. Hence, there are number of rules that must be followed in preaching. Firstly, a sermon must contain some personal experience of a preacher. Its absence makes preaching dry and unrealistic. Secondly, the main purpose of a sermon must be the salvation of human souls. Although edification of believers is important, its main purpose has to be the message of salvation. Thirdly, every sermon must have Jesus in its center. A sermon without Christ is merely the meditations of a preacher, rather than preaching.[68]

Prokhanov also mentions a number of recommendations for a preaching event—preacher's gestures, intonation, appearance, the length of a sermon, the style of speaking, and many others. His final remark, however, was rather revolutionary for his time,

64. Ibid., ch. 2.
65. Ibid., ch. 7.
66. Ibid., ch. 8.
67. Ibid., ch. 10.
68. Ibid., ch. 10.

> The preacher should leave no critical remarks about their sermon without attention, whether they come from friends or enemies. In no situation he should be offended by people's criticism. Instead he should be grateful for that, taking it into account and correcting mistakes. Our critics are out best teachers.[69]

As I will show in chapter 4, preaching gradually became overspiritualized, leaving no space for critical evaluation, which was considered inappropriate or even sinful.

In this section, I have addressed an important and fruitful period in Russian baptistic history. Relaxation of governmental restrictions on the work of non-Orthodox churches led to unprecedented growth and maturity in the baptistic movement. It grew numerically, but, which became very important for the period of severe persecutions, it developed structurally and gained clear denominational identity. Baptists and Evangelical Christians have made significant efforts in developing tools for educating their communities and their leadership. Publications, conferences, Bible schools, all were geared toward one goal: the evangelization of the whole country. With a growing number of educated people, their greater exposure to international community, and most importantly, the vanishing novelty factor of the biblical message proclaimed outside of the traditional Orthodox liturgy, the training of missionaries, pastors, and lay preachers gained paramount importance.

It was a thorny way of laying foundations for theological education. Its proponents not only needed to overcome barriers set by the government officials, but also to win over those pastors and lay members who perceived education, and especially theological studies, as a way to distance people from God, a deviation to the simple way of Christ. However, when most of these problems were overcome and several schools began to function, churches started to appreciate and welcomed their ministry.

Of course, it would be naïve to expect that a short, although intensive, period when a few hundred people received theological training could have completely changed the way preaching was understood and practiced in Russia. Yet it was the start of something big that had the potential to transform both the baptistic movement and, perhaps, the whole country. Unfortunately, another change in governmental policy brought the era of fast growth, freedom, and high hopes for the future[70] to a sudden stop.

---

69. Ibid., chs. 16, 17.

70. Prokhanov's dream of building "Evangelsk," a large city in Siberia, populated

DEVELOPMENT OF RUSSIAN BAPTISTIC PREACHING

Trials and Tribulations:
Living in a Spiritual Desert, 1929-1987

From the moment Bolsheviks gained power in 1917, they openly promoted atheism. However, until 1929, atheistic propaganda was done in a fairly peaceful fashion. It can be compared to a new religious movement that entered the country's religious scene, aggressively competed with the established players, and particularly the Orthodox Church. Of course, the competition was never fair, since the "new religion" was extensively supported by the communistic authorities. In 1929, the government introduced new legislation, clearly aiming at the elimination of all religious organizations, and, moreover, at the destruction of all faiths.

There is no accurate number of how many Soviet citizens suffered as a result of Stalin's repressions. Various sources suggest figures from 800,000 sentenced to death and over 4 million imprisoned, to almost 20 million murdered and nearly 35 million sent to prisons.[71] Christians were among the groups targeted by the state oppressive machine. Most of the sacred buildings were destroyed or converted into shops and warehouses. Pastors, priests, and other religious leaders were arrested and sent to labor camps or prisons in the remote areas of the USSR to serve terms of ten, fifteen, or twenty-five years. In 1917, there were over 141,000 Orthodox priests in Russia. By 1941, over 140,000 were arrested, sentenced to long imprisonment, or killed.[72] A majority of Baptist pastors and active members shared the fate of their Orthodox colleagues.[73] Their families lost homes, could not find employment, and were therefore left without means for survival.[74]

The intensity of persecutions lessened during World War II. Millions were released and rehabilitated (many posthumously) after Stalin's death.

---

primarily by evangelical Christians and governed by God's law, is only one example of the hopes and dreams of the leadership of evangelical Christians. (Prokhanov, *V kotle Rossii*, 225; also Popov, "Khristianskiie komunni," 135–38)

71. For further reading, see Zemskov, "GULAG"; Applebaum, *Gulag*.

72. Pereligin, "Orlovskaia eparkhiia," 343.

73. My grandmother, Lilija Onischenko, shared her memory of living under the oppressive regime. In their church there were Sundays when people had gathered for a worship service, but no one dared to lead the service (the pastor, the deacons, and all the preachers had been arrested by then). The person that started a service, in most cases, would have been arrested the same evening. Cf. Jones, "Baptists and Anabaptists revisited."

74. Prokhanov, *V kotle Rossii*, 246–49.

However, oppression of some sort continued all through the Soviet period. It was inevitable, therefore, that the communistic era would leave multiple scars on the Baptist movement in Russia and other former Soviet republics—heavy and complex heritage that Christians were to deal with after the collapse of the USSR.[75] Without even trying to address a wide spectrum of issues Baptists had to face under the Soviet regime, I will focus on one area of particular interest for this research—Christian education and the preparation of preachers.

Atheistic Academia vs. Baptistic Spirituality

None of the few educational programs that Baptists and Evangelical Christians started at the beginning of the twentieth century could operate after 1929. The government slightly changed its destructive policies in dealing with Christians during World War II. This change was partly forced by Nazi attempts to win the loyalty of the population in occupied territories through allowing freedom of worship.[76] On the other hand, a change might be seen as recognition that brutal force did not achieve the desired results—many people kept their Christian faith. For Baptists and Evangelical Christians, the change resulted in a merger into one union and the beginning of the publication of *Bratskii Vestnik* (*BV*).

It might be necessary to mention that two independent unions of Baptists and Evangelical Christians ceased to exist as a result of the Soviet persecutions. In 1944, and with the permission of the government that was seeking to control the country's religious organizations, the All-Union Council of Evangelical Christians—Baptists (AUCECB) was formed. The congress consultation of the representatives of Evangelical Christians and Baptists took place in October of that year, with a number of its participants being released from prisons prior to the meetings. The congress decided to form one union, appointed its general council, and established a system of senior pastors (starshiie presvitera).

These and some other decisions resulted in the formation of a system which significantly restricted local congregations' ability to make

---

75. See Pavlyuk, "Destructivnoie naslediie sovetskogo proshlogo," 40–45; also Andronoviene and Parushev, "Church, State, and Culture," 161–213.

76. Ermolov addresses the question of the life of Russian evangelical Christians on occupied territories in "Evangelskiie khristiane–baptisti v period okupatsii RSFSR 1941–1944," 174–75.

autonomous decisions, without receiving permission from the leadership of the Union, yet made it easier for the Soviet administration to have greater control of the church. Komarov argues that the formation of the AUCECB and other signs of relaxation of persecutions were nothing but an attempt by the government to create some kind of ministry of spiritual affairs to execute better control of the evangelical movement from within, as other non-Orthodox denominations were also forced to merge with the AUCECB (the Pentecostal church "joined" the AUCECB in 1945, the Mennonites in 1966).[77] Such unification inevitably caused difficulties for congregations, which were somewhat different in their theology and practice. Hence, there is a diversity of opinions on the appearance of the AUCECB through such forceful integration of various denominations into one entity.

Stalin's death (1953) marked an end of militant atheism and the state's new approach to anti-religious oppression, the so-called "scientific atheism."[78] The authorities focused on propaganda among young people, creating a perception that faith and science were in irresolvable conflict. In addition, they introduced practices of public intimidation of children and young people from Christian families, at the same time imposing restrictions and limitations on all church activities related to youth work.[79] The authorities also attempted to discredit Christians by closing access to higher education, and work in such spheres as medicine, education, or art, leaving manual labor in construction, agriculture, and industry as the only possibilities for employment.

Alexey Sinichkin, one of the leading voices in the area of Russian Baptist history, highlights a number of ways the Soviet government attempted to discredit the church through various policies it enforced on the Baptist Union through its governing body (AUCECB and senior pastors), which included prohibition of leading services or performing baptisms for anyone without the Council's approval and accreditation, restrictions placed on youth work, encouragement of the use of church discipline (e.g. excommunication from churches on grounds of un-Christian or immoral living), and many others. In their attempt to control the ecclesial bodies, the authorities even allowed the compilation and publication of the hymn-book

---

77. Komarov, "Evangelskiie christiane-baptisti v sisteme," 194–99.

78. Mitrokhin, *Baptism*, 42–62. For an in-depth description and analysis of Khrushchev's anti-religious policies, see Durasoff, *Russian Protestants*, 192–230; Popov, "Evangelical Christians-Baptists," 74–76.

79. Panich, "Children and Childhood," 156.

in order to bring coherence into the lives of local churches (as well as removal of hymns with ambiguous, and thus potentially inappropriate from the state's perspective, meanings) and a recommendation to focus teaching and preaching on spiritual matters, rather than issues related to everyday living. The governmental department dealing with religious affairs went as far as recommending the authorities to allow Baptists to open a Bible school, which could train pastors who shared values of the communistic state and supported its politics, although this did not happen.[80]

One of the most significant consequences of atheistic propaganda was a widening gap between academia and churches. Historically, Russian churches were more conservative when it came to anything introduced by educational institutions, whether secular or religious, despite a well-known proverbial saying, "Learning is light, whilst ignorance is darkness." I have previously mentioned that the roots of such a perception of formal education can be traced to the period of the Great Reforms, when universities received the reputation of being faithless places of rebellious thinking. Although the efforts of the baptistic leadership at the beginning of the twentieth century to change negative attitudes toward theological training in churches started to bear fruit, Khruschev's atheistic surge on churches rekindled mistrust and even hostility toward formal education. Moreover, from that time, schools and universities were seen as places that cultivated an atheistic worldview, hence young people were discouraged from pursuing higher education.

Nonetheless, despite the challenges churches faced, the authorities could not fully paralyze their activities in training new generations of preachers. Many pastors (some had received training before the persecutions started in the late 1920s) were released from prisons and returned to their churches in the 1950s, giving a major boost to the missionary and educational activities of local churches.[81] Popov notices that it was common for Russian evangelicals to see their worship as a place of education, and many worshipers were used to taking notes during sermons.[82] Listening to sermons was the main way of education, as well as one of the main objectives of learning, since preaching was perceived as the most important skill that any pastor could acquire. Moreover, an ability to preach was considered one of the key skills for all people involved in any ministry—choir directors

80. Sinichkin, "Vlast i sluzhiteli," 155–56.
81. Sawatsky, *Evangelicheskoie dvizheniie v SSSR*, 185.
82. Popov, "Evangelical Christians-Baptists," 161.

preached during rehearsals, and youth workers proclaimed the word at all youth events, including birthdays, weddings, picnics, and others.

The most common way for young people to learn to preach was self-training based on listening and reflection with little, if any, assistance from older brothers. The proverbial saying, "God is teaching his people to preach," was gradually becoming not only the way young people saw their ministry, but also the methodology promoted by pastors.[83] Eventually, in many congregations, it became common for preachers' training to simply consist of asking every male member of a church to deliver a sermon (multiple sermons in every service provided ample opportunities for listening and preaching). Whilst learning through practice is essential when it comes to preaching, such important elements of educational process as subsequent critical evaluation and feedback were hardly ever present, hence severely restricting the potential development of prospective preachers.

Conclusion

In this chapter, I have offered an overview of a complex history of the development of preaching ministries in Russian baptistic communities from its formative period through the years of relative prosperity, freedom, and subsequently fast growth and development, and then to a final period of oppression of the church by communistic authorities. Whilst it is impossible to exhaust the field in a chapter, the exercise is important since it is the first attempt to explore Russian baptistic history through the lens of the development of their preaching. In addition, I was able to highlight some important trends in how preaching was understood and practiced, and how this understanding changed with shifting political realities, thus inevitably leaving a mark on the baptistic communities.

Let me summarize the most important points. Initially, preaching was understood to be the task of every member of the community. It was done in a form of literal interpretation and immediate application of the biblical story to the lives of the listeners. However, the preacher's interpretation wasn't considered to be final or inerrant. Rather, it served as the beginning of a discussion, when listeners were allowed to offer alternative insights, raise disagreements, and ask questions. Preaching was a truly communal exercise!

---

83. Sinichkin, "Vlast i sluzhiteli," 169.

With education becoming more accessible, there was a growing need to bring some theological coherence into the diverse congregations of Baptists and Evangelical Christians, as well as offer training to the quickly expanding numbers of pastors and missionaries. The leadership of the two unions reacted to these challenges by organizing educational opportunities, and through developing publishing activities, which became an important tool for raising theological literacy, providing examples of good quality sermons, and bringing a sense of unity to congregations spread over the vast territory of the Russian Empire. Preaching gradually became the task for people with a special calling and training.

The tragic period of communistic persecution and repression affected all spheres of Soviet society, penetrating and changing the lives of every family. Churches turned into targets for police violence and atheistic propaganda. Gradually, Christians were pushed to the margins of social life, when ordinary people were embarrassed even to admit that someone in their family attended church services. For the church it was a long battle for survival. When all educational activities were disrupted, youth work was prohibited, and social involvement was banned, the only area where believers could successfully resist the oppression was in their spiritual and ethical lives. During that time the churches' main approach to teaching preaching could be summed up in two phrases—to spend more time in prayer and to read the Bible.

4

Preaching and *Bratskii Vestnik*

Introduction

WHILST CHAPTER 4 CONTINUES to explore the history of the Russian Baptist movement and particularly the development of preaching during the period of communistic oppression, its main focus will be on published materials, specifically *Bratskii Vestnik*. The importance of this medium is difficult to overestimate, since until the opening of the Bible Correspondent Courses (BCC) in 1968, the only resources available to churches were publications in the *BV*, which played a significant part in shaping the understanding of various aspects of preaching ministries. However, prior to addressing preaching itself, it might be helpful to start with a wider subject of biblical hermeneutics and exegesis.

Biblical Exegesis in Post-war Publications

The Scripture has always been of paramount importance for Russian Baptists, who learnt to see almost every aspect of their personal and ecclesial life through the lens of the Bible. However, despite the emphasis on the Bible as the source and foundation of Christian faith, the subject of biblical interpretation received surprisingly little attention because of a strong conviction that the Holy Spirit was giving any born-again believer the ability to understand the Scripture. This view may seem not dissimilar from biblical literalism of the first baptistic communities. The difference, however, was in the emphasis on the need for the interpreter to belong to the church, which had the final authority in accepting or rejecting the message, being the only agent that possessed the fullness of the knowledge of the word. Whilst such congregational approval may appear to be a sound practice of communal discernment, in reality the ultimate authority in matters of faith was given to the leadership of local churches. Thus, it was a step away from truly communal reading of the Scripture and toward uncritical reception of any message proclaimed by the preacher.

Ivan Motorin[1] wrote a number of articles on biblical subjects, which appeared in the *BV* from 1946 to 1947. Although his articles resemble sermons both in style and content, they are helpful in shedding light on the role and the use of biblical text. In the article "Bible—the Word of God" the author stipulates that the main God-given criteria for the reader/interpreter is to have a pure heart. The right heart leads to another crucial element of biblical interpretation: the belonging to the church.[2] In turn, the approach to avoid is compared to the work of Pharisees or "modernist theologians," who are people that study the Bible in seminaries and universities, have great knowledge, but miss the most important element: personal regeneration. Since they approach the Bible as a mere ancient text, rather than God's revelation, such method is considered "exceptionally harmful."[3]

Motorin offers a number of alternatives. The most significant aspect of biblical interpretation is that the Bible "should be studied diligently, with especial eagerness and reverence, and most importantly, with prayer." Other suggestions include to read the whole Bible; to study the Bible topically and to read available reference books; to study different sections of the Bible; to make notes, but most importantly to "pray and reflect." Only this allows the reader to "enrich themselves with the divine truth and the knowledge of the eternal Word."[4] Finally, sharing the insights with sisters and brothers is seen as a good practice, since this is the way to deepen one's knowledge of the Bible and to receive necessary corrections, as the fullness of biblical knowledge and of discernment of God's will reside with the "universal Church,

---

1. Ivan Motorin was one of the leaders of the ARUEC. In 1924, he became the leader of the Union of Evangelical Christians in Ukraine. During this time he supervised publications of the journal *Evangelist*. In 1944, he participated in the discussions, leading to the formation of the AUCECB. In 1966, Motorin was elected into the General Council of the AUCECB.

2. Motorin, "Bibliia—Slovo Bozhiie," 4–5.

3. Motorin, "Kak izuchat bibliyu," 58.

4. Ibid., 60.

which is the gathering of the saints."[5] Yet, as Popov notes, "there is little awareness of the universal church beyond the AUCECB, in the concrete historical setting about which he is writing."[6]

Exegetika (*Exegetics*), a handbook of the BCC on exegesis, was the next significant work on the subject of biblical hermeneutics and exegesis produced by the AUCECB.[7] According to the authors of *Exegetika*, the person of Jesus Christ is the key to reading and interpreting the Scripture: "The Holy Scriptures with all its immensity is composed following one plan—to testify about Jesus Christ. Therefore, an exegete must everywhere and always seek and see Jesus Christ, and hold His direction."[8] Most of the Bible is considered to be clear for the readers, "the Scripture should be understood just as it is written, which means all the words should be understood in their common sense, without over-intellectualizing. No doubt, God said in His Word exactly what He wanted to say."[9] The authors recognize, however, that not all passages can be interpreted literally. Hence, the reader of the Bible must be able to recognize different types of meaning of biblical text—literal and spiritual (spiritual meaning can be either metaphorical or prototypical).

The handbook suggested two types of interpretive tools—analytical and auxiliary. Analytical tools include the definition of the purpose of the book or a passage, the meaning of words and phrases, understanding the context and biblical parallelism ("juxtaposition of two or more similar passages of the Holy Scripture in order to explain texts difficult for understanding").[10] Auxiliary resources are information about the author of the book, its characters and purpose, and the time and place when the book was written. It is suggested that most of this information can be gained from the Bible, although additional knowledge can be received from the works of Christian

---

5. Ibid., 60.

6. Popov, "Evangelical Christians-Baptists," 102.

7. The book was written by Alexander Karev (General Secretary of AUCECB from 1944 until his death in 1971; also General Editor of *Bratskii Vestnik*), Artur Mitskevich (Starshii Presviter [senior pastor] of Ukraine [1946–1956], Vice General Secretary of AUCECB from 1956, Director of BCC from 1968), and V. Popov (a pastor of a local church and one of the teachers at BCC).

8. Karev et al., *Ekzegetika*, 4.

9. Ibid., 5.

10. Ibid., 10, 12–17.

theologians from the first four centuries. All of this underlines an important hermeneutical principle—the Bible is interpreted by the Bible.[11]

Similarly to Motorin, the authors of *Exegetika* address the issue of who can interpret the Bible. Their conclusion is that "an interpreter must be a child of God. Only such an interpreter possesses gifts which give him assurance in the work of interpretation." The authors then explain that differences of interpretations, or even disagreements between believers, can occur if there was no true regeneration of the interpreters, as well as due to the diversity of their life experiences and existing differences in the level of their spiritual maturity.[12] As Popov noted, "In practice, the demand of spirituality and holiness in the interpreters meant conformity of their interpretation to ideals, norms, and standards accepted among the 'holy people.'"[13]

Bratskii Vestnik on Preaching

Although the *BV* was one of the key instruments of developing preachers in churches, and despite the importance attributed to preaching, the journal contains a limited number of articles on the subject of homiletics. From 1945 to 1989, there were less than fifteen articles dedicated to the subject of preaching.

It would come as an unexpected surprise to many pastors in Russia, but the first article specifically dealing with preaching addresses the question of the role of women in this ministry. The author insists that since "the spiritual condition of the churches largely depends on the condition of the sisters, the question of female ministry should be considered as very important." The argument against women in preaching based on Paul's prohibition for women to speak in churches as in 1 Corinthians 14:34 is dismissed through a number of biblical references—1 Corinthians 11:5, Philippians 4:2–3, Acts 2:17 and 7:1–6, and Luke 2:38. The author concludes, "All of the above makes it clear that women can serve on the field of preaching the Gospel."[14] The subsequent volumes of the journal do not show a change of attitude to this issue. At the beginning of 1948, Yakov Zhidkov[15] routinely mentions female preachers, "Under the

11. Ibid., 6, 17–21.
12. Ibid., 10.
13. Popov, "Evangelical Christians-Baptists," 110.
14. "O sluzhenii zhenshchin v tserkvi," 48–49.
15. Yakov Zhidkov served as a president of ARUEC after Prokhanov's immigration

guidance of the beloved brother—the presbyter, some gifted brothers and sisters participated by sharing the word of holy Gospel . . . "[16] Indicating that the practice of female preaching was not considered as unbiblical or sinful, which is a prevalent viewpoint in twenty-first century churches. Ten years later, Zhidkov reaffirmed the notion of women in this ministry, referring to the decision approved by the leadership of the Union, "Those brothers and sisters that are gifted and able to teach the church are allowed to preach . . ."[17] Nonetheless, it needs to be noted that the *BV* in its publications always referred to preachers using the masculine pronoun. Similarly, women preachers never featured on its pages.

Other publications can be mostly divided into two categories: dealing primarily with the character of a preacher, or issues related to the sermon preparation. The first is given much more attention, as almost every article contains extensive exhortation on the need to spend time in prayer before, during, and after the process of preparation for preaching, the importance of the supernatural work of the Holy Spirit, and the prophetic nature of preaching. The theme of preaching being more than a mere rhetorical discourse clearly comes to the forefront in every publication. Despite some mild attempts to address practical issues related to the ministry of proclamation, the preachers and the listeners were given a clear message—the right heart of a preacher and his relationship with God are the most important elements for a successful sermon. Therefore, the task and responsibility of the listeners is to come prepared not only to listen, but more importantly to hear God's message.

The two articles by Prokhanov dealing with questions of a preacher's character appeared in 1946. Prokhanov argues that preaching ministries should only be open to those who "meet the criteria set by the Word of God,"[18] otherwise proclamation loses its ability to influence people. The author identifies four qualities that every preacher must possess. The first is *conversion*. The power of personal experience of accepting Christ and turning away from sin is directly linked to the convictional power of proclamation. Without such spiritual experience, biblical and theological knowledge

---

in 1928. From 1932 until 1942 he was in prison for his religious work. In 1944, Zhidkov was elected as a President of AUCECB. In 1955, Zhidkov was elected as a Vice-President of the Baptist World Alliance (re-elected in 1960).

16. Zhidkov, "Vzgliad nazad," 7.
17. Zhidkov, "Poriadok propovedi na nashikh sluzheniiakh," 58.
18. Prokhanov, "Kachestva propovednika," 18.

is considered to be lifeless scholasticism. The *calling* of a preacher, the second important quality, is confirmed by their preaching gifts. This, however, comes from a church, and not from a preacher. The third quality is *knowledge of the Bible,* which is different from "theological theories" and other religious knowledge. Prokhanov believes that every preacher must try to memorize large bits of the Scripture, which also would be a natural result of constant reflection on the Bible and its daily application. The final characteristic is a *preacher's life,* and an urge to be an example for other believers in every aspect of their living.[19]

The editors of the *BV* extensively used Prokhanov's heritage. His sermons, articles, and even his preaching style were set as an example for other preachers. The article "I. S. Prokhanov as a Preacher" is a lengthy analysis of his preaching style, full of flowery metaphors and flattering comparisons (Prokhanov as a preacher was compared with, and considered to be superior to, Spurgeon, Moody, and Torrey). However, this ode to one of the "greatest and most gifted preachers not only of our country, but of all countries in the world"[20] sets a number of important emphases which help us understand what was expected of a sermon. The proclamation of the gospel, understood as a call to repentance, was the first and foremost purpose of a sermon. Although the author indicates that preaching must also contain "food for mind and heart," nevertheless, the examples of the fruits of Prokhanov's sermons were always stories of people accepting Christ as their Savior, asking for forgiveness, and bursting out in public prayers.[21] Therefore a sermon was first of all a tool for evangelism.

The article "Some Instructions on How to Prepare for Preaching" again places significant emphasis on the spiritual condition of a preacher. A preacher needs the help of the Holy Spirit. Without him, no correct interpretation or application of the Scriptures is possible. Therefore, the process of preparation should start and end with a lot of prayer. The author addresses such questions as preparation, reading commentaries (indicating that reading parallel passages is the best way to understand the Scriptures), creating some structure, and following one theme.[22] However, all of it does not distract a reader from the main idea—preaching is a prophetic ministry empowered through the work of the Holy Spirit:

19. Prokhanov, "Kachestva propovednika," 18–21.
20. N. N., "I. S. Prokhanov kak propovednik," 68.
21. Ibid., 68–70.
22. Motorin, "Nekotoriie ukazaniia," 53–56.

After the draft of the sermon is ready, you need to throw it to the feet of Jesus and fall in front of Him. Your notes are just dead bones, which lack flesh and, which is more important—life and spirit, the source of which is in God's hand. Pray to Him that in every moment of your sermon you, according to His promises, were given necessary thoughts in your heart and the words of life were put in your mouth.[23]

Motorin, in "Preacher's Ministry," addresses such problems as powerless preaching and pastors' integrity. He rebukes those who reject preparation on the basis of Matthew 10:19–20, reminding readers that the passage relates to a courtroom, and not to the context of a local church. The recommendations on how to prepare a sermon can be divided into three categories. First, spiritual preparation involves reflection on a specific passage and prayer. Second, stylistic preparation is defined as the need to be aware of gestures, choice of words, intonation, and the general "appropriateness" of a preacher at the pulpit. Those whose character or preaching style do not conform to 1 Peter 4:11— "If anyone speaks, they should do so as one who speaks the very words of God"—are told to be banned from this ministry.[24] And finally, structural preparation consists of using notes, which helps preachers to maintain clarity of thought and direction all through the sermon. Motorin refers to the examples of Prokhanov, Kargel, and Pavlov, "who never preached without notes." Finally, preachers are advised to use publications from the BV.[25]

A year later, a similar piece by Schavelin, a preacher and the author of many publications in the BV, entitled "What a Preacher Must Know," addressed similar issues of preparation (mainly through prayer and meditation), style, and length of a sermon. However, the author placed much heavier emphasis on the supernatural nature of preaching. The main themes of the article can be formulated through the following quotation, "Each preacher must daily, with prayer, immerse himself into the abyss of God's wisdom and guidance ... The preacher who is not in Christ always

---

23. Ibid., 56–57.

24. Motorin, "Sluzheniie propovednika," 43–44.

25. Ibid., 46. Based on this recommendation for preachers to use the BV as a source for their preaching, the subsequent issues of the journal regularly feature such sections as "V Pomoshch Propovednikam" ("To Assist Preachers") and "Misli dlia Propovednikov" ("Thoughts for Preachers"). These sections contained Karev's notes for sermons, offering preachers ready-made materials for their use in churches.

risks in his sermon to deviate from what the Holy Spirit wants."[26] All the subsequent promptings to prepare, be sensitive to the listeners, notice the audience, are not substantiated in any way, thus conveying a clear message: the "right heart" and solid relationships with God will inevitably produce an edifying message, that speaks to the hearts of the listeners, prompting their prayers.[27]

Zhidkov's article, "The Order of Preaching in Our Services," creates a framework for preaching in churches. All the recommendations are explicitly based on the document adopted by the council of AUCECB. The reason for such instruction is stated in the following way: "We have to give guidance to our brothers, involved in the ministry of the Word, so that the churches would receive sufficient amount of spiritual food." First Timothy 4:11 and 6:2–5 are used to provide biblical backing to the abovementioned guidelines, some of which clearly have to be seen in light of the growing pressure from the Soviet authorities in their push to impose greater control over churches. First, it is clearly defined who is allowed to preach: the pastor, the deacons, and some brothers and sisters whose gifts are recognized by the church. These people must be members in their churches as it is inadvisable to allow visitors to have access to the pulpit. Second, criticism of other religious movements or Christian denominations is prohibited. Third, the New Testament should be a primary source for preaching, whilst preaching on the book of Revelation and the Old Testament is discouraged (unless the preacher uses passages "which are clear and do not require especial preparation for their interpretation"[28]). Fourth, the use of stories and personal examples in preaching is commended, yet with a caution—stories must be "appropriate, conforming to the serious spiritual content of a sermon."[29] Fifth, preachers must responsibly prepare with much prayer, "since believers expect to hear from him spiritual word, as from the Lord."[30]

The notion of preaching being primarily a result of the work of the Holy Spirit is further developed in the instructions to pastors. Evgenii Masin compares the ministry of proclamation to the ministry of the biblical

---

26. Schavelin, "Chto dolzhen znat propovednik," 69.

27. Ibid., 69–72.

28. Zhidkov, "Poriadok propovedi na nashikh sluzheniiakh," 59.

29. Ibid., 59–60.

30. Ibid., 60. An article by Spurgeon published in 1958 continued to develop the main idea that "spiritual abilities and . . . inner spiritual life" were the main tools in preacher's ministry, whilst all the hard work in such areas as rhetoric, logic, and knowledge were secondary (Spurgeon, "Rabota presvitera i propovednika," 30).

prophets and the apostles. The prophetic word is "God speaking to the people of God," also it is "the direction to the church, the light that shines in the darkness."[31] Such a high view of preaching is reinforced by Artur Mitskevich in "Priesthood of All Believers and Church Ministers." The instructions on how believers should listen to sermons are worth an extensive quote, because this message has become a regular theme for sermons in churches across the Soviet Union and today's Russia, first of all emphasizing the responsibility of the listeners in discerning the message:

> "Watch, how you are listening,'"—said Jesus in Luke 8:18. Through preaching God performs His gospel seeding. Be watchful, open the ears of your heart, hear and reflect. Be like Mary at Jesus' feet, place in your heart the seeds of eternal life. Do not sleep or doze, so that the evil one would not steal the seed planted in your heart (Matt 13:19). Do not let your heart become a transit road for various unclean or vain thoughts. Find pearls in what was said, wonderful truths, draw lessons not only for others, but also for your personal life. Do not set your heart for criticism or judgment. Reject everything which stands in the way of your reverent fellowship with Jesus, open your heart to Him, to receive new purification and sanctification, new joy and edification, new blessing for the continuation of your journey.[32]

An article by Sergei Fadyukhin, who was a pastor of Leningrad Baptist church from 1966 to 1980, "Recommendations to Preachers," can be seen as a sum total of the previous published materials. It is divided into three parts, each covering an important area of preaching ministry. Like most other preaching publications, it opens with the person of a preacher. The author states that the preacher's integrity and personal experience are paramount for preaching ministry, "We, preachers, have no moral right to speak about something we haven't lived through." The person cannot be a preacher unless he has had a "personal spiritual meeting with Christ" and Christ's personality is reflected in his life.[33]

The good knowledge of the Bible is included in the list of important qualities. This happens through reading and reflecting on the Scripture, and then presenting one's thoughts to "senior, more experienced brothers." Other steps toward deeper understanding of biblical texts include

---

31. Masin, "Presviter dolzhen bit osviashchen Gospodom," 58–59.
32. Mitskevich, "Vseobshcheie sviashchenstvo i sluzhiteli tserkvi," 30–31.
33. Fadyukhin, "Sovety propovednikam," 33–34.

understanding the context in which a particular text was written and reading parallel passages since "the best interpreter of the Bible is the Bible itself." And the purpose of every sermon should be "repentance, revival, and strengthening of faith."[34]

The second part of the article features the term "homiletics" (for the first time in the *BV*), which is defined as developing and honing natural gifts of preachers such as public speaking and clear logical thinking. The preachers are advised on the choice of Scripture texts and advised to use one of three forms of preaching: a verse-by-verse explanation of the biblical text; a verse-by-verse explanation, but with greater emphasis on one main idea; and preaching on a particular theme. The third form is deemed to be the preferred choice, yet also the most difficult one, since it requires a preacher's extensive knowledge of the subject and ability to present his thoughts in a clear, logical sequence.[35]

The final part deals with various questions related to a sermon preparation, such as the choice of preaching theme, understanding the audience, developing sermon notes, the length of a sermon, and the preacher's behavior in the pulpit. However, despite some helpful and practical comments (e.g. the preachers should welcome criticism, as it stimulates their development), the main idea reemphasizes the prevalent spiritualized view of preaching,

> Each biblical text has rich content, for it is God's Word. However, if when you consider it, you see that although this passage is beautiful this beauty seems vague, leave the passage—this is not the text that God wants you to take for your sermon. The text gifted to you from God will be clear for your understanding and deep in its content.[36]

A short summary of the chapter might be required at this stage. I have offered an overview of all the publications of the *BV* on preaching covering the period from 1945 to 1969. Nearly all of them conveyed a rather unambiguous message—the most important thing in preaching is the preachers' spirituality. Personal spiritual experience, passion for Christ, time spent in prayer, reflection on the word, as well as genuine desire to see people saved—these were the main prerequisites for a successful sermon. In turn, the listeners were taught that discovering precious pearls of God's truths was their responsibility when listening to preaching. Active listening (with prayer and

---

34. Ibid., 35, 36.
35. Ibid., 37–38.
36. Ibid., 41.

reflection prior to the worship service) was encouraged, and moreover was made a requirement for a successful sermon. Although the majority of Christian preachers would emphasize the importance of prayer and God's guidance in the process of sermon preparation, the overspiritualization of the practice that can be observed in the publications of the *BV* eventually led to lower standards of preaching in churches, as well as opened the doors for abuse of power since preachers, and particularly pastors, were given special status as *God's* "anointed people," and thus were exempt from any accountability.

The leadership of the Union was aware of the problems. Their dissatisfaction with the state of ministry of proclamation can be seen in publications that attempted to mend poor preaching by engaging with questions of sermon preparation, structure, style of delivery, and by offering sets of sermon notes for use in churches. Nevertheless, most of the recommendations these articles brought forward—such as to have clear structure in sermons, read commentaries, notice the listeners—only highlighted the need to rely on the Holy Spirit in preparation, since no commentaries were available, the correct understanding and application of the Bible was understood to be purely a result of divine revelation, and the listeners were expected to make their own sense of what the preacher proclaimed.

After 1969, there was a period of seventeen years before the next article on preaching appeared in the *BV*. In order to understand such an apparent gap in dealing with an important issue, it would be helpful to address some of the matters the AUCECB had to face. The sixties turned out to be turbulent years for the Baptist Union. The approval of the controversial by-laws and the instructional letter to senior presbyters in 1959 was the opening of a Pandora's box.[37] As noted by Karev, "The storm that started in

---

37. Under the pressure of the Soviet authorities, in 1959 the council of the AUCECB adopted two divisive documents, "Polozheniie o Soyuze Evangelskikh Khristian–Baptistov v SSSR" ("The By-Laws of the Union of Evangelical Christians-Baptists in USSR") and "Instruktivnoie Pismo Starshim Presviteram" ("Instructional Letter to Senior Presbyters"). Although these regulations, imposed by the Soviet authorities, clearly attempted to restrict the church growth, they were approved and sent out to local churches. Some of the most controversial points were as follows: local churches were excluded from the election of the members of the General Council of AUCECB, prohibition to the *senior presbyters* to participate in worship services on their visits to churches, a suggestion to restrict baptisms for people under thirty years of age, effectively a ban on evangelism and calls to repentance during worship services, prohibition for individual Christians to participate in any religious activity outside of the registered church premises, and rejection of people who were baptized by pastors/evangelists not recognized by the AUCECB. The introduction of these documents and rules caused a split in the AUCECB and the emergence of the independent Baptist Union—the Council of Churches. In 1963, these

August 1961 surpassed all previous expectations." The split in the Union, the dissent of hundreds of churches and thousands of believers caused a significant shortage of qualified pastors and preachers. Several newly appointed senior presbyters had neither sufficient training nor experience. Hence, there was a growing number of churches with problems caused by leaders abusing power and doctrinal dissidence.[38]

The leadership of the AUCECB saw part of the solution in offering theological education and ministerial training to its pastors and lay members. In 1964, they applied for permission to publish 10,000 Bibles and to open BCC, which was granted. The first educational institution of the AUCECB began to operate in February 1968. The majority of the 100 students that were enrolled in the program had various roles in their churches—senior presbyters, pastors, deacons, preachers. The two-year course included such disciplines as doctrinal theology, introduction into the Old and New Testaments, homiletics, exegesis, history of Christianity, history of Evangelical Christians-Baptists, and others. Until the opening of Odessa Theological Seminary in 1989, the BCC remained the only educational institution of the Baptist Union, with over 1,000 students graduating through their program.[39]

Nineteen seventy-one brought another major change. Aleksei Bychkov was elected as a General Secretary of the Baptist Union after the death of Karev. Popov noted,

> The death of Karev meant a complete shift of generations among the ECB leaders. Pastors who had seen the evangelical revival of the 1920s, had survived the Great Purge,[40] and had laid the foundation of the AUCECB, were now succeeded by ministers raised during the post-war period. The new board of the AUCECB consisted of leaders for whom the Union of Evangelical Christians-Baptists was the only form of the evangelical movement they

---

by-laws were annulled, and at the AUCECB congress in 1966 the leadership of the union issued public repentance. Nevertheless, until the present moment, the relationship between the churches of the Baptist Union and the Council of Churches has not been fully healed. (*Istoriia evangelskikh khristian-baptistov v SSSR*, 240–41)

38. Ibid., ch. 7.

39. Ibid., ch. 7.

40. "The Great Purge" (also known as "The Great Terror") is a term that refers to a wave of political repression in the Soviet Union that occurred between 1936 and 1938. This time is known for the mass arrests, imprisonments, and murders of the members of the Communistic Party, the Red Army, and every other social group in the country. For further reading, see Conquest, *Great Terror*.

knew. On the one hand, the new leaders venerated their ancestors as those who had succeeded in raising the brotherhood from ruins to relative prosperity twice, after the October Revolution and later after World War II. Thus they showed extreme conservatism in almost all spheres of life, notably worship style.[41]

The conservatism that Popov refers to resulted in almost a total absence of educational materials in the *BV* from 1971 to 1988. The lack of theological education of the Union leadership caused increased emphasis on the value of spiritual formation, even at the expense of theological training, which is clearly observed in preaching.[42]

Conclusion

This chapter provides a conclusion to a section that addresses a complex subject of the development of preaching in Baptist communities over three distinct periods in Russian Baptist history—the formative years, the period of fast growth, and a much longer era of trials and tribulations. At all these stages, different external factors made the church adjust its theology and practices to the changing cultural and political environment. At the formative stages, baptistic preaching was characterized by heavy emphasis on moral living and projection of biblical narrative into the life of communities and individual Christians, as well as criticism of the Orthodox Church. This was important as churches were learning to use the Bible as the main source for their faith and practice. The period of freedom and fast growth brought forward the need to bring coherence into the teaching of local churches. The need was addressed through extensive publishing activities by Baptists and Evangelical Christians. Spiritual articles, sermons, and theological materials were also used in preaching. Theological and ministerial training was of prime importance, and was rapidly developing despite various barriers set by the authorities.

Spiritual formation and personal piety came to the forefront again during the time of persecution. The church lost its educational institutions, and suffered a great loss of pastors and preachers. In such difficult times, *BV* became the main source of theological and educational materials for congregations across the Soviet Union. I have shown that most of its articles on preaching presented biblical interpretation, and more specifically ministry

---

41. Popov, "Evangelical Christians-Baptists," 85.
42. Ibid., 179–80.

of proclamation, as an impossibility without due spiritual preparation. Although some practical aspects of sermon preparation and delivery were noted, nonetheless it can be said that the journal played an important role in making preaching into a practice where the preacher's spirituality was given far more weight than any other aspect of this ministry. In churches, such views led to a situation when being a preacher first of all meant being an exemplary Christian who spends a sufficient amount of time with God and the Bible. Gradually preachers were lifted to a special place of honor, as people especially close to God. The pulpit by itself became a sign of God's special calling and anointing.

5

Preaching in Contemporary Russian Baptist Churches

Introduction

THE PREACHER'S SPIRITUALITY, THE authority of the pulpit, and the listeners' attitude to proclamation are the main subjects of chapter 5. I will argue that preaching plays a far greater role in churches than that of mere educational or inspirational speech. Preaching is as much about teaching the Bible as it is about authority, which this ministry yields to its practitioners. Unfortunately, the questions of power and authority are neglected in the discipline of homiletics, thus inevitably contributing to tensions and conflicts between churches and educational institutions in Russia. This claim is based on my previous exploration of the historical and theological contexts in which baptistic churches have emerged, as well as the analysis of the practice of proclamation in contemporary churches, which is the subject of this chapter.

The Context of Worship

Worship Pattern

The absence of rigid liturgy, extemporaneous prayer, and preaching with the anointing of the Holy Spirit were the characteristics that attracted many people to the baptistic churches at the early stages of their development. However, despite this positive experience in history and often-repeated claims that Baptists do not have traditions, Baptist worship in Russia may turn out to be as rigid as an Orthodox liturgy. The order of service does not differ much in various places around the country. Moreover, as I shall demonstrate below, the pattern of worship has not significantly changed over the past hundred years.

It might be possible to distinguish several types or patterns of corporate worship services among Russian Baptists: regular service, prayer gathering, Eucharist, outreach event, and a service with a special event like baptism, ordination, wedding, or prayer over children.[1] The differences between these services are insignificant. For example, a prayer gathering is almost identical to a regular worship service. The main differences are in sermons pointing to the importance of prayer and motivating Christians to pray for a certain cause; music aiming at creating a reflective and meditative atmosphere; and time slots for extemporaneous prayers of the worshipers being extended, allowing anyone wishing to pray out loud an opportunity to do so.

Since the differences between various types of services are often focused on details like the selection of hymns, the focus of sermons, and sometimes the number of sermons, focusing on a regular worship service would be the most helpful, as it presents a core pattern around which certain changes are occasionally introduced. The traditional pattern of worship service would be as follows: the service begins with an opening prayer (in case of a major holiday like Easter the opening words could be holiday greetings), which is followed by a congregational hymn. Depending on the size of a congregation and the scale of their music ministry, the opening hymn might be followed by a choral or orchestral piece. According to Irina Timchenko, a music director from a Baptist church in Moscow, the type of service influences the choice of this first hymn, which can either be a hymn prayer or a triumphant choral.[2]

The first sermon (traditionally fairly short, up to twenty minutes long), as a rule, is delivered either by a guest or a beginner preacher. In many churches, this sermon is named a call to prayer. It is always followed by extemporaneous prayers from members of the congregation, followed by a choir piece, congregational hymn, and often by several smaller performances, such as solo singing, an orchestral piece, a testimony, or a poem. The second sermon is usually a general exhortation on Christian living and

---

1. Timchenko, "Muzikalnaia osnova bogosluzheniia," 70.
2. Ibid., 71.

is preached by an experienced preacher. The sermon is followed by an interlude consisting of choral, congregational, or solo singing. The donations can be collected at this point.

The main pastor of the church or another respected minister is responsible for the final sermon. Often this preacher tries to summarize previous sermons, and often, if necessary, *corrects* the preceding speakers. Clearly, the degree of their correctness is defined solely by that last preacher.[3] As a rule, the final sermon concludes with a call to repentance, often reinforced by an appropriate choir piece. At the end of the service there is time for announcements, and greetings are passed to the church from other places. Finally, a short benediction is said, traditionally "The Grace" from 2 Corinthians 13:14.

The pattern of the abovementioned worship service suggests there are many active participants. Various kinds of musical pieces, testimonies, poems, and of course multiple acts of preaching require numerous church members to be involved. Moreover, when three or four weekly services are added to the picture, it becomes obvious that churches that follow this pattern have to have many people taking part. So, who can be involved? With music ministry it is rather simple—anyone. The only requirement is that a person is neither on church discipline[4] nor leading a particularly sinful way of life, since everyone who leads worship has to provide a positive example for others. This occasionally raises an issue of whether nonmembers (or nonbelievers) can be involved in music ministry at all. However, in most cases, baptism and church membership are not viewed as a prerequisite for joining a choir or a praise band. Poetry and testimonies are also open to

---

3. A young pastor from a small congregation in the Voronezh area once told me that preaching the last sermon in every service was the main principle of his preaching ministry. Such an approach allowed him to ensure that people leave the church with "correct biblical theology." Ironically, this pastor never received theological training, and most of his preaching was aimed at denouncing sin and temptation. It was the pastor and the deacons who decided what was to be labeled as sinful—for example, one of their youth leaders was banned from participation in ministry because he worked as a waiter at a restaurant. In this case, preaching the last sermon was understood to be a powerful instrument of control available to the pastor and not anyone else.

4. In Russian Baptist churches, "being on church discipline" means that the person is not allowed to participate in the Eucharist and business meetings of church members until he/she repents of the committed sin and restores broken relationships with the church. Unfortunately, the practice is often used as punitive, aiming at the elimination of sinful behavior (this includes both sins mentioned in the Bible as well as any other type of behavior that is considered sinful by a particular community, and can include such areas of life as clothes, places of work, and many others). Cheprasov, "Church Discipline," 93–94.

everyone, both men and women, both baptized members and those who have just started their walk with Christ.⁵

The Ministers of the Word and the Problem of Authority

Unlike music ministry, to be a preacher one has to meet two conditions. Firstly, a potential preacher has to be a man.⁶ Secondly, he has to be a baptized member of a Baptist church in good standing. Often, these are the only conditions for a person to be offered an opportunity to preach. To be a preacher does not require formal theological education, as preaching is seen not as an activity that involves training and preparation, but rather as a responsibility of every Christian man.

The discussion about worship leaders must include Popov's point about the existence of "a special class of believers called "sluzhiteli" (ministers)."⁷ The word derives its meaning from the verb "to serve." However, this concept has a more complex connotation, making it difficult to explain to people outside Russian Baptist culture.⁸ *Sluzhiteli* are not pas-

---

5. Kargel's views on the relationships between the believer and the Holy Spirit might be helpful to gaining an understanding of the expectations of the church in relation to people involved in ministry. Kargel speaks about the role of the Holy Spirit in giving the believers "the power from on high," which is required for the life of the disciples, enabling them to be Christlike. Any obvious sinful acts, like lack of love or compassion, cruelty or desire to be praised—are clear indications of the person not living with the Holy Spirit. Kargel insists that being filled by the Holy Spirit is a necessary requirement for believers, since it produces a desire to serve others, sharing with them everything that was given by God. ("V kakom ti otnoshenii," 124, 133)

6. In the previous chapter I have already touched upon the subject of female preaching. Historically Russian baptistic pulpits were open to women. Sadly, the majority of contemporary Baptists have drastically changed their attitude toward women in preaching and in pastoral ministry—this is now generally perceived to be sinful and unbiblical. It is difficult to trace the roots of such changes, however through the surveys collected from various churches I noticed that the majority of older preachers (without formal theological training) affirmed female preaching, which nevertheless has never been common in Russian baptistic communities. Most of the categorically negative responses were received from pastors and preachers less than 40 years of age, mostly with at least a Bachelor degree in theology. This raises a question on how the contents of the educational programs that developed in the post-Soviet countries influenced their attitude to this issue.

7. Popov, "Evangelical Christians-Baptists," 259.

8. This difficulty points to an important issue of language barrier, which is one of the negative consequences of the enforced separation of the church from social life during communistic oppression. For helpful insight, see Pavlyuk, "Destructivnoie naslediie

tors, although pastors and deacons are a part of this group. *Sluzhiteli* are involved in ministries of local churches, yet their main characteristic is first of all their exemplary spiritual life. Popov notes, "(T)hese ministers were considered as a spiritual elite, consisting of a few chosen ones in the congregation. The status of sluzhiteli had to be won by personal qualities and recognition by church leaders."[9]

The concept of *sluzhiteli*, most of whom are involved in the ministry of proclamation, brings up a notion of authority and its connection to preaching. Yuri Sipko, who served as a president of Russian Baptist Union from 2002 to 2010, whilst maintaining a positive image of *sluzhiteli*, who are "entrusted with the building up of the saints,"[10] indicates that various abuses do happen. Answering the question "Why unwritten laws of the brothers (*brothers* is another term used as a synonym to *sluzhiteli*) are sometimes more important than the Holy Scripture in Baptist churches?,"[11] Sipko points to several issues. First is the lack of critical engagement with the Bible, both among the preachers and the listeners. He argues that once a church had formed its theological position on various biblical and moral principles, it became intolerant to anyone questioning these views. The second contributing factor is the threatening and oppressive environment where Baptists existed and developed, which resulted in the withdrawal of Christian communities from the wider society, and the subsequent development of a sense of mistrust or even hostility to the outsiders.

Finally, Sipko refers to a culturally accepted authoritarian approach to leadership, "Tsarist style in the state, in society, in churches, results in formation of leaders' holy immunity. The leader does not err!"[12] According to Sipko, this is both imposed *from above*, being taught by church leaders, and supported *from below*, with laypeople treating pastors as God's anointed servants. All of it highlights a serious problem: for a church leader to accept that he might be mistaken means "to accept his inadequacy and to lose face."[13] Inevitably, these pastors/preachers rarely hesitate using such arguments in their teaching and preaching as "obedience is better than sacrifice . . . this is accepted practice in the brotherhood . . . you simply need to

---

sovetskogo proshlogo," 41).

9. Popov, "Evangelical Christians-Baptists," 259–60.
10. Sipko, "Zhit' po biblii," para. 6.
11. Ibid., para. 1.
12. Ibid., para. 13.
13. Ibid., para. 14.

listen."[14] People who dare to disagree or criticize the practices or views of such leaders are called heretics, or labeled as traitors. Sipko concludes that such pastors have usurped the right of the whole church to read, understand, and interpret biblical truth.[15]

The notion of the preacher's authority is extensively developed by David Brown in *Transformational Preaching*. Adapting Max Weber's concept of charismatic, rational, and traditional causes of authority,[16] Brown presents three sources of a preacher's authority. First is "anointed authority," which "resides in the character of the individual." This is where the preacher may speak about the divine calling for their ministry. Second is "attributed authority," which is "granted, by the institution," for instance when a local church or a denomination appoints someone for a particular position. The third type of authority is what Brown calls "assumed," which is "authority that emerges from within the preaching event itself. It resides fully in the person who is fulfilling the role, but only while in that role."[17]

Brown emphasizes that for their ministry to be persuasive, preachers must be recognized by their listeners as having authority to speak, particularly if preaching is understood as a prophetic ministry. At the same time, he points at a number of potential dangers in dealing with the issue of authority. A preacher's integrity becomes extremely important, as strong Christian character serves as a guarantee against a threat of preaching being used as a tool to manipulate the listeners. In this sense, the prominence given to preachers' individual ethics and spirituality in Russia appears to be a much-needed antidote. On the other hand, together with preachers' integrity, Brown highlights the vitality of educated listeners, who provide the necessary accountability for the people in the pulpit.[18]

Now, this second element is often missing from the equation, leaving both the prophets and their listeners vulnerable and unprotected from the potential abuses of power. Moreover, instead of learning to read the biblical story afresh, without the strangling lenses of the tradition, enabling regular church goers to become the practitioners and interpreters of the word, the church establishment often plays a negative role, suppressing sincere questions, emphasizing the value of traditions (even those without biblical

---

14. Ibid., para. 15.
15. Ibid., para. 18.
16. Weber, *Theory of Social and Economic Organizations*, 324–423.
17. Brown, *Transformational Preaching*, 239–47.
18. Ibid., 243.

authority, like prohibition for women to preach). This specific view of leadership as people anointed by God, and which allows a lot of space for mystical direct involvement of the Holy Spirit in the lives of the believers through participation in a holy event of worship and listening to the word, further contributes to the formation of "ministerial holy immunity."[19]

Nicolai Kornilov, a professor of history at MTSECB, makes an important observation about the nature of biblical authority in churches. He argues that although the church teaches that people have to believe the Bible, in reality, people are taught a set of convictions defined by their leaders, which is very similar to the teaching of the Orthodox Church: "believe everything that the church is teaching you."[20] The lack of engagement of ordinary members with the biblical message, and substituting it with some mysterious "teaching of the church" poses serious problems for the witness of such congregations. Kornilov notes,

> When the Bible is given in an ideological wrapping, as a solution to all grieves and problems, it becomes very dangerous. This is because if it does not work as such solution, it is instantly rejected. Or this would lead to fanaticism. Apart from this, any ideology quickly loses appeal in Russia. This includes biblical ideology . . . That is why we, Christians, are the first reason for the destruction of biblical authority. First, we do not know it (the Bible). We do not study it. We only quote it, use it to cover up our opinions and preferences . . . This is a source of the second problem: the lack of understanding (of the Bible) forces us to preach what is on the surface, what we are used to. But we do not speak from the Bible, we do not respond to people's needs. That is why our preaching is empty . . .[21]

Although I do not assume that all or even the majority of preachers in Russian Baptist churches can be rebuked by the abovementioned articles of Sipko or Kornilov, their points must be taken seriously. Whilst the typology of the sources of preaching authority suggested by David M. Brown helps us get a better understanding of the multifaceted concept of authority and power in churches, a significant theme should not be omitted—the call for *educated listeners*, able to evaluate the message proclaimed from the pulpit and hold preachers accountable. This latter element is often left out of

---

19. Sipko, "Zhit' po biblii," para. 13.
20. Kornilov, "K voprosu ob avtoritete," 14–15.
21. Ibid., 34.

the ecclesial scene, thus leaving churches without a vital tool of protection against abuses of power.

Contemporary Understanding of Preaching

Addressing the question of contemporary understanding of preaching in Russian Baptist churches, it might be helpful to say that initially I have approached the subject of formative preaching in a similar way to many other educators, who attempted to teach preaching in Russia. I was interested in such questions as how people listen to sermons. What do they remember after the preaching event? What rhetorical devices are appropriate in the pulpit in a given cultural setting? Thus, I have started my research by collecting a number of surveys from several Baptist churches in the Voronezh area, which was supposed to be the first step toward conducting similar surveys in churches across the Russian Federation.

However, the responses that I received created a complex picture, bringing various important, yet unexpected issues to the forefront, eventually steering my research from a study on homiletics to approaching preaching as a social practice, which needs to be considered within Russian historical and theological contexts. Further research on the subject has revealed that views and understanding of preaching that surfaced from the surveys is a natural outcome of how preaching in Russia has been developing. Thus I decided to limit my survey to one region, which will be used as a case study that, based on the findings of the preceding chapters, can be seen as largely representative of Russian Baptists.[22]

I have collected 100 surveys from four churches in the Voronezh region. I aimed to have a variety of congregations included in order to see whether the location, the age of the congregation, and patterns of service that are followed affect the way people understand preaching and what they expect it to be. Thus, I approached a city-center congregation that follows traditional patterns of worship and preaching with approximately 400

---

22. I am not attempting to do quantitative research, although I have included respondents from various age groups, educational backgrounds, and Christian experiences. Neither should the use of percentages of people who responded in various ways be an indication of my attempt to do statistical analysis of the views of preaching thar are prevalent in Russian Baptist communities. The use of the opinions of the respondents from the Voronezh area was instrumental in directing my research toward historical and theological analysis of how preaching evolved. At this stage, the summary of the results of the surveys serves as an illustration that is based on previous historical and theological study.

members. The second one was a community with approximately 130 regular worshipers, founded nearly twenty years ago in a suburb of Voronezh. The third church was started twenty-five years ago, and now is a similarly sized congregation with young adults constituting two thirds of it. The church is located in the city of Voronezh. The fourth church, a fairly young congregation, planted approximately ten years ago, also has a high proportion of young people, although it follows a traditional style of worship and preaching. Current membership of the church is over ninety people.

The surveys included preachers (nearly 40 percent of all respondents; all male), and nonpreachers, men and women of different age groups. The received responses in most cases did not seem to depend on the age or gender of the respondents, which serves as another confirmation of my previous claim that the existing understanding and form of preaching in Russian Baptist churches has deep cultural, theological, and historical roots. Let me try to summarize the findings of the survey by way of an expanded definition of what preaching is understood to be.

First, preaching is seen to be a vehicle which brings the written word of God into the lives of the listeners. This happens when the Holy Spirit speaks through preachers. It is worth noting that the border between the written word of God and the proclaimed word is rather blurred. Preaching is both the Bible explained, but also God speaking through the preacher.

Second, the results of sermons are up to God because he works in acts of proclamation. Preachers believe that they should have no defined goals for their sermons when entering the pulpit. The only result that preaching must hope to achieve (indicated by nearly 60 percent of the preachers) is conversion, which is also the result of the work of the Holy Spirit. Hence, all the preacher should do is allow the Holy Spirit to work.

Third, there is no bad preaching. For the majority of the respondents a sermon is a mystery. This idea features in one way or another in over 80 percent of all the surveys. True preaching starts "on the knees," meaning in prayer, as some pastors like to remind their flock, and is fully dependent on God. Such understanding explains why those people who have belonged to a church for a long time are afraid to be critical about preaching. Some of them have even corrected my survey by crossing over questions: "Are there bad sermons?" and "How often do you hear bad sermons in your church?" Instead they wrote phrases such as, "Preaching is a result of God's work, it cannot be bad." Such an attitude is best illustrated by the following statement, affirmed by both preachers and listeners: "If you do not find the sermon edifying, something is wrong with your heart."

Let me expand this point a little further. The questions related to bad preaching were answered by the nonpreachers (sixty-two people in total) in the following ways:

Thirty-seven people firmly stated that preaching cannot be bad. Only eight people in this group were under fifty years of age. Thus, the majority of those who view preaching as the supernatural activity of God, which therefore cannot be criticized, are people over fifty years of age, who have been members in Baptist churches for over two years. They see their spiritual immaturity or the "hardness of their hearts" as main reasons for some sermons "not touching them."

Twelve people said that there were too many bad sermons, which was defined as speeches lacking structure and meaning that was a result of preachers' insufficient education or preparation. However, these people also believe that "God can use even bad preaching to change people's hearts."

Thirteen people believed that although there are some bad sermons, this is often caused by preachers not investing enough time in prayer and preparation, since preaching by itself cannot be bad, being in its essence the work of the Holy Spirit (This last point is a contradiction in itself, yet such conflicting views are not unusual when people share their convictions about church and faith.[23]).

Among the preachers (thirty-eight respondents), the attitude toward bad sermons is slightly different. Fourteen preachers believe that preaching is always good, being a result of divine activity. Eight indicated that there are many bad sermons. Sixteen preachers are convinced that if a preacher does not invest enough time in preparation he should not expect a sermon to succeed.

Preachers who are over fifty years old generally have high regard for preaching. They adhere to the view that preaching cannot be bad, being the word of God. Preparation for the act of proclamation is, first of all, a spiritual exercise for preachers' hearts and minds, which involves prayer and a good knowledge of the Bible. Younger preachers (twenty to forty years old) frequently express dissatisfaction with the quality of preaching in

---

23. Lingenfelter and Mayers argue that the main difference between Western and Eastern thinking is that the latter is not preoccupied with building logically coherent structures or systems. Instead various narratives, facts, or convictions are allowed to be independent, thus allowing for the peaceful coexistence of seemingly conflicting stories/beliefs (*Ministering Cross Culturally,* 52).

churches. However, their concept of preparation differs from viewing it as a purely spiritual exercise. Rather, they emphasize a rigorous understanding of biblical text achieved through the use of commentaries, being in favor of expository preaching popularized by John McArthur.

Let me add a bit more complexity to this already intricate issue. As I wrote earlier, effectively 80 percent of nonpreachers and 70 percent of preachers believe that preaching cannot be bad (with some allowance for the poor spiritual preparation/condition of the preachers). Nonetheless, nearly 75 percent of all the respondents denied that they agree/trust everything they hear from the pulpit. In addition, the majority of respondents, including those with a very positive view of preaching, were able to identity problematic issues—whether the sermons frequently were too long, lacked structure or clarity, or simply were not relevant.

Leonid Mikhovich highlights various reasons for a preaching ministry to cause dissatisfaction among church members. These are: the poor preparation of the preachers, both spiritual and biblical, the lack of gifted preachers, and the inability of pastors to say "no" to willing church members who have no calling to this ministry. All of this is possible due to the need to have many preachers because of the numerous worship services with multiple sermons. The lack of qualified preachers results in sermons being irrelevant to the lives of the listeners, lacking spiritual depth, and, which is equally important, having no passion (when it comes to delivery). Nonetheless, the author points out that although the abovementioned weaknesses reduce the effect a sermon can produce, people believe that even weak sermons bring God's blessings, since God's power is revealed in weakness. Finally, many people learnt not to expect too much of sermons—they listen to quality preaching on radio or television, but come to a public place of worship to meet other Christians, to be present in God's house, and to listen to his words (every sermon contains a lot of biblical material).[24]

Conclusion

The ministry of the word in the eyes of many listeners is first of all the ministry of the Spirit, which has the power to transform people's lives. Preachers, therefore, are viewed as anointed ministers, called by God to the building up of his church. As such, their ministry should not be critically examined or criticized. This strong conviction of ordinary Christians not

24. Mikhovich, "Compatibility of Theology and Practice."

challenging those anointed by God is cultivated by some church leaders. A long-standing emphasis on a person's spirituality as the key to correct biblical interpretation has further advanced the notion of preachers (the interpreters of the word) as being members of the Christian elite and superior to others in their closeness to God.

A second important contributing factor in preachers receiving special treatment is inherently present in the Orthodox culture, where preaching is seen as the instrument of divine presence. The role of the listeners, therefore, is to come with their hearts prepared for a sacred event. The balance of heart or mind, emotions or reason, is an important question when persuasive discourse is concerned. In the Russian context heart and emotions take priority. Believers are invited to humble themselves, repent of their wrongdoings, and allow God to work. For the majority of worshipers, such qualities as humbleness and a repentant heart exclude the spirit of criticism.

Speaking about the audience, it would be wrong to say that ordinary members in Russian churches are biblically illiterate. People generally know the Bible well. However, their ability to go beyond literal understanding of biblical passages is rather limited. Popov wrote,

> The beliefs of the ECB concerning the Bible defined the methodology of Bible studies. The principles of simplicity and holiness implied that spiritual (not intellectual) development was the key to a correct understanding of sound biblical teaching. As a result, these evangelical believers treated education in general and Christian education in particular with great suspicion because, in their opinion, it was likely to be an attempt at forgery—an attempt to forge genuine spirituality. For them true spirituality could be reached only through personal holiness, which could be achieved through deeper fellowship with Christ.[25]

Thus, despite people's ability to freely quote biblical text, it is still possible to speak about the absence of "educated listeners, able to hold preachers accountable."[26]

Due to various reasons mentioned earlier in this work, such as political oppression and a somewhat forced emphasis on spirituality, the pulpit—after being the initial catalyst of the baptistic movement—became a sign of special anointing and authority for the chosen few, consequently limiting the right and desire of ordinary members to read and interpret the Scripture.

---

25. Popov, "Evangelical Christians-Baptists," 110.
26. Kornilov, "K voprosu ob avtoritete," 14–15.

Individual theologies of the church leaders became a major factor in shaping all aspects of Baptist ecclesial life. Pastors turned into sole arbiters who defined preachers and sermons as appropriate or heretical, edifying the church or disrupting the congregation, as well as making decisions regarding worship practices, social ministries, and even matters of everyday life for their members. Therefore, the lack of accountability and the absence of the congregation that could reflect critically and theologically on sermons or certain church practices, played major roles in the appearance of various abuses, eventually leading many churches to lose young people, and even to the general loss of denominational identity. Contemporary Baptists in Russia, as well as other post-Soviet countries, find it hard to explain who they are and why they do what they do. The revivalist movement that aimed to reshape all areas of Russian society has turned into a religious institution with rigid structures, practices, and traditions.

6

The Need for a Vision
Defining Baptistic Identity

Introduction

IN THE PRECEDING CHAPTERS I have shown how proclamation played a major role in the formation of the first baptistic congregations, who were forced to leave the Orthodox Church largely due to their conviction that everyone needed to study the Bible and apply it to their lives, being guided by the Holy Spirit. Through various stages in their development, these believers maintained a very high view of the ministry of the word, which they perceived as a direct work of God. The years of persecution and oppression under communistic regime, when churches were forcefully separated from all aspects of social life, resulted in distortions in how churches understood their role and place in society, and created various tensions and challenges within the congregations.

Newly gained freedom after the collapse of the USSR and the almost immediate spread of educational institutions that produced thousands of graduates in theology, revealed the discrepancy between the alleged need of more trained pastors and preachers and the reality when local communities were unwilling to accept and use people with qualifications in theology. The pneumotological approach to ministry appropriated by churches effectively excluded the need for education, which was perceived as a threat to authentic spirituality.

Preaching was rather central to such church-seminary conflict, since churches considered proclamation as their key instrument for forming and maintaining the spirituality of their members. However, there was little to no reflection done on the meaning of these terms, nor did such an approach help solve the problems these congregations were facing in the rapidly changing world around them. Educational institutions identified preaching as one of the crucial areas of the church ministry that needed reforming, yet they attempted to do that without contextualizing their methods (effectively neglecting questions of Baptist identity), and by reducing preaching to the disciplines of hermeneutics and rhetoric.

My argument is that instead of being perceived as a mere rhetorical act with some spiritual or educational value, preaching has to be seen as a powerful practice. Churches and educational institutions need to recognize its constructive and destructive potential in order to preserve and maintain baptistic identity, and to enable a more fruitful relationship between the church and the university, thus leading to the much-needed transformation of the contemporary Russian Baptist movement.

This brings me to the main question of this chapter, the issue of baptistic identity. To define the characteristics of a church that can be called baptistic, I will employ the concept of the Baptist vision as developed by McClendon, and in particular his thesis that what makes Baptists a separate ecclesial type is a particular guiding vision, a specific way of reading the Bible. I want to stress that the approach I am taking views identity as something robust and coherent around the vision.[1] Thus, the subject of this chapter will be to define a target culture by focusing on a vision that makes Baptists distinct from other Christian types, the vision that impacts their convictions and practices, the vision that is actualized through a certain way of communal and individual living.

Various Ways to Define Baptist Identity

In Russia the question "Who are Baptists?" commonly will have two responses. The outsiders may say that this is a church/sect where people do not drink alcohol, do not smoke, and do not swear. Such a definition may be rooted in the emphasis Baptists always place on holy living, which traditionally was first of all associated with abstinence from alcohol, tobacco, and places of entertainment, such as restaurants and theatres. Remarkably, however, is the fact that many Baptists are not able to provide a much sounder definition. Frequently they opt for a negative identity, attempting

---

1. Parushev, "Walking in the Dawn," 107.

to explain who they are by pointing at what they are not, thus supposedly exposing the shortcomings of other denominations (such as the veneration of icons of the Orthodox, or glossolalia of the Pentecostals).[2] Douglas P. Sharp notes that Baptists find it incredibly difficult to define their identity, due to their diverse historical backgrounds and contexts.[3] He refers to William H. Brackney's point that some Baptists trace their origins directly to Jesus or even better, to John the Baptist; others link themselves to the Anabaptists; still others are convinced that every time the Holy Spirit forms a church, that church should be classed as Baptist.[4]

This inability of Baptists to define who they are can be partly explained by the absence of any authoritative creed, or even a set of doctrines that distinguishes Baptists from all other Christians, which in itself is one of the baptistic principles.[5] For instance, Edgar Y. Mullins argues that because the voluntary principle is the core principle of Christianity, the right of "private judgment in religion" is the core right of Christian faith. A Baptist, therefore, can never judge the representative of another denomination on the basis of any creed, since every person is free to exercise religious freedom.[6] Hence, when Baptists try to enforce their interpretation on other Baptists, it means that they themselves have moved away from what can be called authentic baptist.[7] The fact that different baptistic groups adopt slightly different confessions and the absence of one universal creed shows that this road to defining baptistic identity leads to a dead end.

When dealing with the subject of identity, various historians and theologians (despite their use of different terminology, such as "Baptist identity," "Baptist way of doing church," "Baptist vision," "Baptist beliefs," etc.) point to a list of hallmarks which are either shared with other Christians or unique to Baptists. Fisher Humphrey, whose work serves as a good illustration here, points to eight major beliefs that all Baptists share: believers baptism; baptism only by immersion; believers' church is a result of believers' baptism; autonomy of the local church; democracy inside the church in discerning God's will; cooperation between local

---

2. Cherenkov, "Nash baptism."
3. Sharp, "Kto takiie baptisty segodnia?," 106–7.
4. Brackney, *Baptists*, xvii.
5. Tuck, *Our Baptist Tradition*, 24.
6. Mullins, *Baptist Beliefs*, 7.
7. Tuck, *Our Baptist Tradition*, 24.

churches for better witness; the church is separated from the state; and no creed but the Bible.[8]

Whilst there are certain benefits of developing an approach to the subject of baptistic identity by providing an explanation of who Baptists are or are striving to be, any attempt to define the borders of baptistic culture by identifying a set of beliefs neither answers how these markers of baptistic identity came into being nor explains why different Baptist churches have slightly different sets of core convictions. Therefore, another way of identifying Baptists is needed that should be neither a historic identity nor a baptistic way of doing church, which implicitly refers to practices and beliefs. Instead, it might be helpful to use another term, a guiding vision, which carries a sense of moving forward, yet leaving space for a variety of contexts and cultures. This search for a vision does not reject attempts to single out baptistic identity by pointing at their distinctives, but asks what causes them to be different. Hence, this is an attempt to discover convictions that precede visible implications of baptistic beliefs. Now, since identity is formed through participation in social life,[9] reviewing and analyzing community practices may serve as a mirror that reflects real convictions of that community.[10] Therefore, with my next step I will tell a story of a community that existed in the first half of the twentieth century.

A Story of the Dobrovolets (Volunteer) Community

The history of the Baptist movement in Russia has attracted a lot of attention in recent years. However, although more work has been undertaken on previously neglected territory, such as the lives of various churches, regional associations, and even individual pastors and missionaries, most research is still focused on people who are considered to be the apostles of the Russian Baptist movement such as Kargel, Prokhanov, Pashkov, and a few others. The number of works written about them will continue to grow as historians discover new material and as state archives are being gradually opened. However, less significant events and people are often forgotten. There is a scarcity of historical material on smaller churches and people who did not become famous preachers or missionaries. Since Russian culture has always

---

8. Humphreys, *Way We Were*, 48.

9. The concept of identity development through social interaction is developed by Berger in *The Social Construction of Reality* and *The Sacred Canopy*.

10. McClendon, *Biography as Theology*, 19.

been primarily an oral culture; the stories that were told in particular communities died with those who kept them. Being persecuted throughout their existence, Baptists nonetheless preserved a missionary zeal, and were more interested in saving souls and surviving the oppression than in writing books. In addition, people did not see themselves as significant enough to leave a record.[11] Finally, in many small communities, a conviction that the Bible was the only important book and that Christ would come very soon were theological reasons for not leaving any written records. In the few following paragraphs, I will offer an insight into a forgotten story of a Baptist community from the Voronezh area.

World War I provides the starting point of the narrative. During the war, a young Russian solder, Peter Leschev, was taken to Germany as a prisoner. His life over there would have made a fascinating story, which unfortunately will never be found. What matters, however, is that he became a Baptist while in Germany and brought this new faith, as some people called it, back home to the village of Ivanovka. Leschev was very enthusiastic about his faith and kept telling people about God and salvation. His witness was rather successful—his seven brothers and one sister, as well as their families, were soon baptized as believers. A small Baptist congregation from a nearby village, Semidesiatnoie, provided spiritual support for this newly established community. In 1921, the Leschev, Popov, Chernich, Ziablokov, Kukuev, Demidov, Cheprasov, Scherbakov, Chekmarev, Rukin, and Smol'ianinov families (approximately seventy people), prompted by the desire to live "according to the teaching of Jesus, and to be like the first church" decided to create a Christian commune or brotherhood.[12]

They lived in separate homes; however, they had common property and a community purse. The commune owned a lot of land where they had built twenty-five new homes for its members, three mills, a smithy, and granaries. In addition they had widened the river and planted large gardens.

---

11. The story I am going to use can be a good example of such "insignificance" of their history in the eyes of its participants. The story of the *Dobrovolets* commune bears personal significance to me, since this is a story of my family. Two of the participants—Peter Leschev and Timofey Cheprasov—are my great-grandfathers. Nonetheless, neither of my grandmothers ever mentioned their story to me, until after I started to work on this project. Apparently, they had never thought their life stories were of any importance.

12. Personal interview with Maria Lesheva (Voronezh, 02.10.2007). Prokhorov mentions that when NEP (New Economic Policy) was introduced by the Soviets in the 1920s, many baptistic communities formed their own "Christian businesses" (*Bozie and kesarevo*, 225). The case that I refer to is different, since the main reason for the appearance of the commune was not business interests, but the desire to live biblically.

The Need for a Vision

In 1926, the brotherhood bought three tractors. Some of their members went to study mechanics, accounting, and agricultural technologies. Nicolay Shutkin, a historian from Voronezh, whose family lived in Ivanovka but was forcefully moved when his parents were imprisoned during Stalin's persecutions in 1930s, notes that this was the first commune in the Voronezh region. It prospered financially due to their hard work and honesty and thrived socially, having "their own system of bringing up children."[3] Various members had different skills, which they contributed to the life of the commune in different ways. "All the fruits of their labor were shared among all the members, no one had shortage of anything," remembers Alexandra Cheprasova.[14]

The commune existed and prospered for about ten years. After the Soviet government started collectivization,[15] in 1931 the commune was turned into a collective farm called *Dobrovolets* (Volunteer). For a while, it continued to exist under a different label, without changing the way they lived. Their members still worked together. Their work was accompanied by singing Christian psalms and hymns, and every day was concluded with a an open-air worship service with all the villagers participating. In the late 1930s, communist repressions began. Several families followed their husbands/fathers who were sent to prisons or labor camps in distant parts of the USSR. Some member families were killed in World War II. Others moved into the city of Voronezh. Many outsiders, including a number of fanatical communists, deliberately moved into the village and joined the collective farm, radically affecting the dynamics of communal Christian life.[16] Shortly after the end of World War II, when two more families were arrested and sent to serve their prison sentence in Siberia, *Dobrovolets* ceased to exist.

Let me touch upon some preaching themes and the role of the Bible in the commune, particularly at the later stages of its existence. Since having a Bible was prohibited by the Soviet state, the adult members kept their Bibles hidden. Their study often took place at night in the fields or in the forest, where they gathered in groups or in pairs to read and reflect on

---

13. Shutkin, "Selo Ivanovka," 57–58.

14. Personal interview with Alexandra Cheprasova (Voronezh, 10.10.2007).

15. Collectivization was a process of the formation of collective farms, when independent farmers were invited or forcefully brought into it. Those who disagreed were robbed and either killed or imprisoned. Thus thousands of people died in prisons and concentration camps of forced labor and malnutrition (e.g. Khlevnyuk, *Politburo*, ch. 1).

16. Personal interview with Alexandra Cheprasova (Voronezh, 10.10.2007).

the Scripture. Maria Lesheva, whose father was the founder of the commune, said that she had never actually seen him reading the Bible. More than that, she had never seen the Bible in the house.[17] Nonetheless, the Bible was read and studied. Biblical stories were preached and narrated to children and young people.

Some stories were so vivid that even eighty years later, they were remembered by those who heard them. The story of the second coming of Jesus meant that everyone was to be ready for his arrival. Being ready did not mean to have right relationships with God, but first of all to live according to his word. The life according to God's word included the fear of rejecting or betraying Jesus (the stories of Judas or Peter became the stories of many who rejected Christ when faced with a threat of death or robbery by communists), which was relevant at the time, when it was dangerous to be a believer. Following the narrow way that led to eternal life was another story. The way of Jesus required purity of heart, which was a life of obedience to God in every aspect, total self-denial and readiness to sacrifice. Suffering and even death were considered a normal part of Christian life. Jesus' command to love their enemies, made the members of the commune welcome anyone, including staunch communists. The words about obedience to the authorities led to hard work as the only way to prove they were good citizens of the Soviet state. The story of the first church sharing their possessions became a foundation for their experiment of communal living.

One of the most prominent narratives recalled in the community was the story of Exodus. To reach the promised land the children of Israel had to have pure hearts, to trust God, and to follow him through the narrow path of temptations. This was the story of Russian Baptists. The story of perseverance going through the spiritual desert of communist rule, leading them into the promised land of God's kingdom.[18] The story of Exodus was a story of people who, despite all hardships, followed God, a story that helped Christians in *Dobrovolets* survive by emphasizing the importance of faithfulness at any cost. What enabled such reading? The understanding of the Bible as their book, the reading of the biblical stories as their story, and perceiving biblical characters not only as real people who lived in the past, but seeing themselves being described by the biblical authors. James Wm. McClendon, Jr. called this "the plain

---

17. Personal interview with Maria Lesheva (Voronezh, 2.10.2007).

18. This account is based on personal interviews with Alexandra Cheprasova, Maria Lesheva, and Lilija Onischenko.

sense" of Scripture that allowed the church to continue to read the text, understand it, and apply it to their lives.[19] Of course there were abuses and misinterpretations, and there were occasional extremes, still this allowed the church to survive and persist in its witness.

This story of Voronezh Baptists brings out a key issue for understanding the baptistic vision: the importance of the Bible, its literal reading, and its application to the lives of the members of the community is emphasized in almost every attempt to define the baptistic way. From the first communities of Stundists to the first Baptist church in Tiflis and gatherings in aristocratic palaces in St. Petersburg, the uniting feature of all these diverse groups is the position and the role of the Scripture for their lives and worship. The reading of the Bible was the discovery of the story of these people, their lost story. An attempt to recover that narrative and live it out resulted in the formation of Baptist churches in Russia.

A word of caution is needed here. Sometimes, extreme biblical literalism leads churches into troubles. Situations when the Bible is raised to the position of self-sufficient god appear for one reason: when the Scripture is perceived as a book that tells us how "we can be made right with God. Personal salvation and justification by grace through faith are the essence of it all and anything else is a matter of indifference or, worse still, law."[20] Therefore, the role of the Scripture is reduced to some historical value, allowing its readers to find out about Jesus and his death and resurrection, and, possibly, to discover what people need "to be saved." Moreover, because the prescription of how to be saved and other important doctrines cannot be easily distilled, or because they can be discovered only by an educated minister who can then teach and preach them to their flock, even though highly respected or worshiped, the Bible loses its real transformational power. There is no reason to read something one either doesn't understand or cannot apply. Thus, the Scripture becomes effectively removed from the congregational life.

Nevertheless, in spite of all the possible extremes that Baptists can slip into, baptistic biblicism turns from "worshiping the book" to being people who live by this book. The whole of life has to be affected by it. The Bible becomes the book where they discover the way to live as a community of believers. This book is written for the church to follow, truly functioning "as a congregational textbook, source of sermons, classroom handbook,

19. McClendon, *Doctrine*, 36.
20. Wright, *Free Church, Free State*, 2.

devotional guide, practical norm."[21] Such a baptistic vision serves as a hermeneutical tool that encourages reading the Bible not as a distant historical account, but as something people can relate to.

The Baptist Vision

The previous section ended with a suggestion that a baptistic vision is a particular hermeneutical principle. Now, it would be useful to turn to a theologian who has grounded his systematic theology in such an understanding of the baptist vision—James Wm. McClendon, Jr. I am far from arguing that his perspective on the way baptistic Christians read the Bible is unique. However, what is unique about McClendon, and is one of the major reasons for referring to his trilogy *Systematic Theology*, is his conviction that this particular way of reading the Bible is the guiding stimulus that has been playing the main role in shaping baptistic communities.[22]

Ethics, the first volume of McClendon's *Systematic Theology*, begins with the quest for a baptist vision. The main reason for having such a starting point comes from McClendon's definition of theology as "the discovery, understanding or interpretation, and transformation of the convictions of a convictional community, including the discovery and critical revision of their relation to one another and to whatever else there is."[23] By understanding theology as a study of the convictions of a convictional community, the first question to be answered is how to define the borders of this community. Thus the question turns into a quest for a theological center, an organizing principle for baptistic theology, which can be seen as a starting point in defining the community of reference, whose convictions and practices a theologian is going to discover and possibly transform.

McClendon reviews several generally accepted marks of baptistic communities—biblicism, mission, liberty, discipleship, and community. However, he argues, none of these hallmarks can serve as a cornerstone for baptistic theology. Thus he offers another approach. He accepts biblicism as the key starting point in defining the vision. However, this biblicism is different than simply a literal understanding of the Scripture, since the authority of the Bible and its normative nature is shared by all Christian traditions, and is not something uniquely baptistic. McClendon claims that

21. McClendon, *Doctrine*, 35.
22. McClendon, *Ethics*, 2nd ed., 33.
23. Ibid., 23.

The Need for a Vision

the Bible can be a starting point in this quest if we consider the difference in the way the Bible is read and applied—only when it works as a "link between the church of the apostles and our own."[24]

Notice that by looking for a vision McClendon does not simply look for a practice or a belief that is inseparable from a particular denomination, but for a conviction that serves as a source of all the others' convictions and practices. As noted by Curtis W. Freeman, McClendon's baptist vision "is not so much a denominational, historical, or sociological account as much as it is a theological standpoint."[25] Thus, the key to understanding baptistic convictions is neither a practice of baptism, nor mission or discipleship. These are practical implications of this vision.[26] According to McClendon, the vision that serves as the key to understanding baptistic theology and is the center of the baptistic way of life can be expressed in the form of a hermeneutical principle:

> shared awareness of the present Christian community as the primitive community and the eschatological community. In a motto, the church now is the primitive church and the church on the judgment day; the obedience and liberty of the followers of Jesus of Nazareth is our liberty, our obedience, till time's end.[27]

In short, the vision is expressed in a motto "this is that" and "then is now."[28] "This is that" is a quotation from the King James Version of the Bible (Acts 2:16) that McClendon uses as an example of how a suggested way of reading and applying the Scripture is rooted in the Bible. In the narrative of the day of Pentecost, when God poured the Holy Spirit on the disciples, transforming them from cowardly people into a courageous group of Jesus' messengers, Peter proclaimed to the people gathered in Jerusalem who

---

24. Ibid., 30.

25. McClendon, *Ethics* (reprint version), xiii.

26. McClendon, "Baptist Vision," 32.

27. McClendon, *Ethics*, 2nd ed., 30. Robinson similarly argues that Scripture is authoritative and formative because the readers can have the same religious experience as biblical characters. In this, Baptists differ from other Christians, for whom scriptural authority lies primarily in its ability to issue right commands, directing to salvation. For Robinson, the Bible is not a "text-book," but a "source-book," allowing believers to live through the written story. (*Life and Faith of Baptists*, 7–18)

28. Recently Harvey has argued that the cupola "is" in "this is that" motto carries certain ambiguity about the immediacy of connecting with the primitive church if applied forcefully. In his view, McClendon's formulation has to be viewed as similitude "this as that" ("'This as That,'" 36–52).

heard the disciples speaking in different languages, that the events described by the prophet Joel were happening that day. He used the phrase "this is that" to relate the phenomenon to the prophecy. McClendon argues that the fact that the prophet might have been referring to different events, maybe even for his own time,cannot reject or nullify Peter's claim as the device when "one set of events and circumstances is applied under divine guidance to another set of events and circumstances" is repeatedly used in the Scriptures.[29] Randy Hatchett argues that Baptists found multiple narratives of evangelism and conversion in the book of Acts that later helped them overcome persecutions and directed their mission efforts. He particularly emphasizes that Paul's conversion, as described in Acts with its themes of meeting the resurrected Jesus and subsequent witness and sufferings, was something like a *type-story* for Baptists.[30] The previously used example of Russian Baptists identifying themselves with the biblical people of the Exodus narrative serves as another illustration of this approach.

"Then is now," is the eschatological part of the vision, is directed into the future.[31] It sees the church of today as the church of judgment day and seeks the Holy Spirit in directing the church into the future. The important emphasis to be made here is that this vision looks both backward and forward as a prophetic vision, a pattern that has been used by baptistic Christians throughout their history.

The existence of such a vision explains why Baptist communities cannot have a rigid creed—they read the Bible not as a book with propositions or rules, but as a story. The story, which is always new, because the people that are reflected in it are always changing, passing through different places in their journeys. "This is that" is a powerful way for people to see themselves, and make the old story relevant for their immediate life. The eschatological dimension, "then is now" adds something to the vision, which makes continuous contextual interpretation and reinterpretation possible. This is the prophetic element of the vision, the understanding that the Bible is not enough for the life of the church. She needs the Holy Spirit to interpret the story from the past into the story of their future, turning mere history into

---

29. McClendon, *Ethics*, 2nd ed., 32.

30. Hatchett, "Hermeneutics of Conversion," 34–35. For more examples of using the biblical story as a type-story, see Randall, "Eastern European Baptists," 15.

31. Leonard speaks about eschaton as a paradox, since "it is at once present and future." ("Eschatology," 206–7) Cf. Moltmann, *Church in the Power*, 192.

an open-ended eschatological narrative.[32] Therefore, the vision provides not only an approach to reading the Bible, but also a way to be followers of Jesus since it is "marked by a textual immediacy—a sense that Christ is present and speaking to the assembly through the Scripture."[33]

Conclusion

Human convictions are formed through participation in the life of the community. With Christians, it is a Christian community that contributes to the development and formation of their convictions, particularly convictions about God, Christ, church, and moral convictions[34] concerning how they should relate to the world outside the church. The practices are rooted in the Scripture that is read as the story of the church, used as a mirror, reflecting the contemporary situation as well as the way into the future. Naturally, believers read it through the lenses of their convictions formed by their Christian community and secular communities to which they belong.

Living together in a community of a local church and as separate individuals influences baptistic reading and understanding of the Bible producing practices that result in certain convictions. Life experience inevitably affects the Bible reading. However, Bible reading also helps believers interpret their life story, to understand themselves in a different way, producing changes in what they believe and do. This is how the vision works—the Bible is read in a context, always anew, being continually reinterpreted and interpreting its readers. Theology in this case is about discovery of what the community (and its members) believes through the examination of their practices (including the practices of reading their sacred story) and the world they live in. After such critical evaluation of these practices in the light of the biblical message, there is a call to something new through challenging the old ways, through maintaining the vision as a way into the future under the Lordship of Jesus Christ.

---

32. Parushev, "Baptist and Society."
33. Hatchett, "Hermeneutics of Conversion," 37.
34. On baptistic vision creating a conventional moral space, see Bakker, "Convictional Theology," 81–97.

7

Practices

Actualizing Resources of the Vision[1]

Introduction

JESUS' PUBLIC MINISTRY STARTED with the calling of the disciples. They were invited to leave their professions, friends, and families responding to the Messiah. Matthew 4:18–22 emphasizes the immediacy with which Peter, Andrew, James, and John answered the call, since for Matthew, discipleship is about intentional participation.[2] The church then became a community of faithful individuals, obedient to Christ's teaching and committed to one another, trying to reflect in their shared lives the story of their Savior. Hence, Christianity is, first of all, a way of life. The words of Jesus, "I am the way, and the truth, and the life," (John 14:6) are a constant reminder of this simple, and yet often challenging truth. And whether believers take the Way as something that follows salvation or constitutes salvation does not change the important emphasis on transformed living.

However, discipleship does not end with the transformation of one's life. Walking in Jesus' footsteps is not a lonely venture. Upon entering the Way, an individual does not step on an empty highway—many others are already there to share the joys and difficulties of the journey. Entering the Way is about becoming a new creation (2 Cor 5:17), joining a new peoplehood (1 Pet 2:9), entering a political reality, which requires active

---

1. The phrase comes from Brown, *Transformational Preaching*, 403, where it is used in reference to the rhetorical materials used by a preacher.
2. McClendon, "Practice of Community Formation," 90.

involvement in the lives of other people.[3] McClendon defines this kind of life by offering an image of three distinct but inseparable and interwoven strands—*body ethics, social ethics*, and the *eschatological vision*. He argues that "the connecting link between the body ethics and social ethics . . . is to be found in the body of Christ that is the gathered church," because it is in a community of believers that Christians learn to live, walk the Way, and witness to the world.[4] Therefore, the existence of the church with its traditions and practices at least partially answers the question of how Christian identity is passed—through involvement in a community and by participating in its practices.

Church practices receive their meaning from the biblical story. The "This is that" part of the vision serves as a pattern that verifies the practices of the church, making the story that Christians are part of visible. Nonetheless, despite its importance, communal practices cannot stand alone. Different themes or motives of the story (which does not constitute the whole story, but only part of it) being embodied in practices may rebel against the rule of Christ by claiming ultimate importance in the eyes of its practitioners. This does not mean that the church will turn into some sort of anti-Christ. Yet, it is a warning that a reductive view of the Bible, the inability of the church to see its sacred story as a whole, is a kind of rebellion or failure by itself. Thus the requirements are set for the eschatological part of the vision, "then is now," the part that focuses on the risen Christ, who is the center of Christian faith. However, since we can only learn about the real Jesus through the Scripture, the question of practices of reading the Bible gains remarkable importance.[5]

What follows is a focus on the concept of practices, particularly as developed by Alistair MacIntyre. His overall positive assessment of practices will be viewed in light of John H. Yoder's understanding of principalities and powers, with a conclusion that practices can be positive, resulting in virtues, and negative, producing vices. This will bring me to McClendon's idea of powerful practices and, subsequently, preaching as one of them.

---

3. Yoder, *Body Politics*, vii.
4. McClendon, "Practice of Community Formation," 86–88.
5. McClendon, *Ethics*, 2nd ed., 47.

Social Practices

In the article on MacIntyre's method in Christian ethics, Nancy Murphy noted that his concept of practice "is an especially illuminating contribution to understanding the Christian moral life," as it may serve as a helpful inroad into the discussion on which practices are central for the sustaining of a Christian community.[6] Brad Kallenberg proposes the existence of several categories of subpractices that form clusters contributing to community formation: witness, worship, works of mercy, discernment, and discipleship. He also argues that participation in these practices is essential for involvement in the tradition called Christianity.[7] McClendon similarly addresses the subject of practices and community formation by naming Eucharist, the covenant meal, as a formative practice of the New Testament church; forgiveness then becomes a skill required for the continuous existence of the community of individuals from a variety of backgrounds.[8] All of the above points to the importance of the concept of social practice for this project, which addresses a practice that is attributed a leading role in shaping the identity of a community—the practice of preaching.

MacIntyre defines "practices" as:

> any coherent and complex form of socially established cooperative human activity through which goods internal to that form of activity are realized in the course of trying to achieve those standards of excellence which are appropriate to, and partially definitive of, that form of activity, with the result that human powers to achieve excellence, and human conceptions of the ends and goods involved, are systematically extended.[9]

Following this definition, a football game, medicine, or marriage are practices[10], and the difference between a practice and an activity (e.g. playing football vs. hitting a ball) is in its purposefulness.[11] This makes the range of practices almost endless as "arts, science, games, politics in the Aristotelian sense, the making and sustaining of family life, all fall under

---

6. Murphy, "Using MacIntyre's Method," 31.
7. Kallenberg, "Master Argument," 22.
8. McClendon, "Practice of Community Formation," 92, 102.
9. MacIntyre, *After Virtue*, 187.
10. Ibid., 187.
11. McClendon, *Ethics*, 2nd ed., 173.

the concept."[12] MacIntyre further explains the concept of practice with the example of a child learning to play chess. At the beginning, the child can participate in the game without having any interest or desire to play, being tempted only by a candy, a payment he is offered. However, a time may come when the child gets the point of the game and starts enjoying the process. This example introduces two further concepts: *goods internal* and *goods external*. The child that plays for a candy may be tempted to cheat, as this candy constitutes the good external. In real life the good external of the chess game can be money, fame, prestige, etc.[13] However, the practice of playing chess also possesses good internal, which is both the enjoyment of the game and the ability to understand its usefulness, which can only be achieved through direct participation.[14]

The good internal, acquired through participation in a practice, is a good that belongs to the whole community, pointing to the formative nature of a practice—participation in a practice produces a virtue, "an acquired human quality the possession and exercise of which tends to enable us to achieve those goods which are internal to practices and the lack of which effectively prevents us from achieving any such goods."[15] In other words, a virtue is an element of an individual/communal identity—making a certain way of life possible.

This highlights the importance of narrative. Narratives provide contexts, which fill actions with meaning. Kallenberg notes that it is "the story of one's life" that "unifies actions into sequences and sequences into a continuous whole."[16] For Christians, such story becomes the narrative they read and understand from the Bible. Thus Hauerwas argues,

> The church says to us, "We're not giving you a story that you can choose. You don't get to make God; God gets to make you. You are made by being brought into this community through which you discover your story. And your story is that you have been created to praise and glorify God—all moral life derives from that truth.

---

12. MacIntyre, *After Virtue*, 188.

13. Campbell uses an example from his seminary of the practice of preaching being corrupted when students of homiletics started to compete for better grades and the financial benefits that came with it, to argue that if "external goods become the focus, the practice is actually harmed." (*Word Before the Powers*, 137)

14. MacIntyre, *After Virtue*, 188.

15. Ibid., 191.

16. Kallenberg, "Master Argument," 23.

Therefore, there is a distinct difference between you and those who have not been made part of God's story."[17]

Such understanding of narrative helps to introduce a concept of tradition—"an historically extended socially embodied argument, and an argument precisely in part about the goods which constitute the tradition."[18] Kallenberg identifies three components of the tradition. Firstly, tradition has a story. Every community "has its continuity,"[19] despite it constantly losing and receiving new members. Therefore, every new member enters an ongoing history, becoming part of it. Secondly, tradition is socially embodied, which means that it only exists when there is a community that chooses to shape its communal life according to a particular authoritative/sacred text. As this authoritative text is being read anew in every generation, traditions penetrate time, being extended through several generations, which is a third component.[20]

Christ and Power

Before continuing to develop the notion of practices, it might be necessary to introduce a concept of power—an issue that cannot be neglected when questions of identity or character formation are addressed. Thus, in the next step I will turn to the concept of powers and principalities as presented in works by John H. Yoder and Walter Wink.[21]

For Yoder the concept of powers does not hold immediately negative connotations. Referring to Colossians 1:15–17, he argues that powers were part of God's good creation, his divine gift to humanity, and despite their fall they are still needed to maintain order and prevent chaos.[22] Like Hendrikus Berkhof, Yoder agrees that the concept of powers is incredibly broad since it includes religious, social, and political structures. Wink argues that powers are not "invisible demonic beings flapping around in the sky,

---

17. Hauerwas, "Christianity," 524.
18. MacIntyre, *After Virtue*, 222.
19. Kallenberg, "Master Argument," 24.
20. Ibid., 24–25.
21. For further development of the concept of "powers and principalities," see Dawn, "Biblical Concept," 168–80; and her critique of Wink's reductionist view of the role of Christ in the defeat of the fallen powers in *Powers, Weakness, and the Tabernacle*, 18.
22. Yoder, *Politics of Jesus*, 140–41.

occasionally targeting some luckless mortal with their invisible payload of disease, lust, possession or death."[23] Instead they need to be seen as

> the inner and outer aspects of any given manifestation of power. As the inner aspects they are the spirituality of institutions, the "within" of corporate structures and systems, the inner essence of outer organizations of power. As the outer aspect they are political systems, appointed officials, the "chair" of an organization, laws— in short, all the tangible manifestations which power takes. Every Power tends to have a visible pole, an outer form—be it a church, a nation, or economy—and an invisible pole, an inner spirit or driving force that animates, legitimates, and regulates its physical manifestation in the world. Neither pole is the cause of the other. Both come into existence together and cease to exist together.[24]

This complex understanding of powers as created by God and thus necessary for the existence of human society, despite being fallen, therefore causing injustice and suffering instead of God planned wholeness,[25] and still not without hope of redemption and restoration through the ministry of Jesus, is well summed up by Yoder:

> (All these structures) can be conceived of in their general essence as parts of a good creation . . . *We cannot live without them.* These structures are not and never have been a mere sum total of the individuals composing them. The whole is more than the sum of its parts. And this "more" is an invisible Power, even though we may not be used to speaking of it in personal or angelic terms . . .
> But these structures fail to serve us as they should . . . They harm and enslave us. *We cannot live with them.* Looking at the human situation from within, it is not possible to conceive how, once unconditionally subjected to these Powers, humankind can ever again become free. . . But nonetheless it is in this world that we have been preserved, that we have been able to be who we are and thereby to await the redeeming work of God.[26]

Yoder develops the notion of the redeeming work of Christ in relation to the powers, arguing that to defeat the fallen powers, Christ submitted to

---

23. Wink, *Naming the Power*, 4.

24. Ibid., 4.

25. Campbell argues that the main goal of the fallen powers is to survive at any cost. Thus, their God given purpose is being sidelined and rejected. (*Word Before the Powers*, 25)

26. Yoder, *Politics of Jesus*, 143.

them just like every human has to. However, Jesus "broke their rules by refusing to support them in their self-glorification; and that is why they killed him."[27] The cross, therefore, becomes the natural outcome of Jesus' resistance to the demonic rule of the powers, highlighting the ongoing struggle for Christians in choosing between preserving life (by siding with the powers) or losing it (by choosing the way of Jesus, and risking ending up with him on the cross).[28] Thus Yoder refers to Berkhof, concluding that,

> By the cross (which must always, here as elsewhere, be seen as a unit with the resurrection) Christ abolished the slavery which, as a result of sin, lay over our existence as a menace and an accusation. On the cross He "disarmed" the Powers, "made a public example of them and thereby triumphed over them . . ."
>
> The weapon from which they heretofore derived their strength is struck out of their hands. This weapon was the power of illusion, their ability to convince us that they were the divine regents of the world, ultimate certainty and ultimate direction, ultimate happiness and the ultimate duty for small, dependent humanity. Since Christ we know that this is illusion. We are called to a higher destiny: we have higher orders to follow and we stand under a greater protector.[29]

The triumph of Christ results in the formation of the church, the transformed community of disciples that are called to represent Jesus through their lives. The church must be a viable alternative for the society, offering life under the guidance of the Spirit, liberated from the corrupt powers of the world.[30] Yoder wrote, "The church must be a sample of the kind of humanity within which, for example, economic and racial differences are surmounted. Only then will it have anything to say to the society that surrounds it about how those differences must be dealt with."[31]

The idea of the church being a prophetic voice in a society, while at the same time showing God's solution to the ills of the world, can be a good concluding point to a work on social ethics, church and politics, or any other field where there is some kind of juxtaposition of the way of Christ and any alternative that leads in the opposite direction. However, when the

---

27. Ibid., 144–45.
28. Campbell, *Word Before the Powers*, 48.
29. Yoder, *Politics of Jesus*, 146–47.
30. See also Harrink, *Paul among the Postliberals*, 118–19.
31. Yoder, *Politics of Jesus*, 150–51.

subject of the research is the church herself and her practices, the idea of powers becomes ever more important. There is a danger of false dualism, perceiving the church as an agent dealing with matters of spirituality and thus being immune to the issues of power, which are relevant to such areas as politics or economics, and thus lead to believers' "blindness to how culture powerfully shapes the inner lives of persons and churches."[32]

Throughout history, there are many examples when the church failed to fulfill its task of freeing persons by providing them with an alternative vision, Christ's way, which is different from the toxic narratives of the world such as nationalism, chauvinism, hatred, greed, and envy. Churches were guilty of genocides, apartheid, and slavery, of embodying the evil structures that Christ came to defeat. Therefore, one of the most important tasks for the church is to continue to identify the fallen powers and to engage them (without complacency), whether they are outside of the church or right at the center of its convictions and practices, which is a revisionist theological task.[33] Hence, this discussion of the concept of power once again brings out an important conclusion: whilst continuing to witness to the world about the redemptive power of Christ, being his prophetic voice, the church must be aware of the dangers of turning her practices and teaching into one of those self-glorifying powers that Christ came to defeat.

Powerful Practices

MacIntyre maintains a positive view of practices, that they are concerned with the goods internal and result in virtues. However, he leaves a caution by differentiating between practices and institutions. Institutions are concerned with external goods, such as money and power, which they use to sustain both themselves and practices. Institutions are an evil, though a necessary one, because practices and institutions are locked into unbreakable union—one cannot exist without the other, and yet the goodness of the practice is susceptible to being damaged by institutions. This is why virtues are important; they resist the "corrupting power of institutions," and "enable evils to be overcome, the task to be accomplished, the journey to be completed."[34]

---

32. Stassen, "New Vision," 214.
33. Ibid., 220. Cf. Wink, *Engaging the Powers*, 84.
34. MacIntyre, *After Virtue*, 194–95, 175.

At this point McClendon suggests a correction, arguing that institutions should be also identified as practices.[35] And since every practice is connected to power (and therefore, is subject to perversion), it can not only produce virtues, but also result in vices. This introduces the term "powerful practice," which originates from McClendon's understanding of the concept of principalities and powers. Beginning with the Old Testament, he shows the inseparable connection between gods and nations in the worldviews of ancient people, linking gods with their social life. Then he moves toward a theological struggle of ancient Israel: How to be the nation of the God called JHWH? In the New Testament he points to the powers as being created by God, yet disobedient and rebellious (including Israel's religious leaders who opposed Jesus, and demonic forces that brought disease and despair into people's lives). Such perception of powers yields a particular understanding of the mission of Jesus as challenging and defeating these powers through his life, death, and resurrection.[36]

The church could continue applying the concept of principalities and powers not only to the external agents, such as the persecuting state, but also to practices internal to Christian tradition, such as the Mosaic Law. This challenge of applying the concept of powers to Christian practices raises an important question: What relations do the practices of the church have to the concept of principalities and powers? McClendon argues that these concepts are related. Christians continue living in the world where degenerated powers are dethroned but not destroyed. This reality defines the missionary task of the followers of Christ to witness that "these civil, military, economic, traditional, cultural, social, yes, religious and other structures are not themselves the end and meaning of life," thus bringing hope of their full restoration according to God's plan.[37]

The Christian life is embodied in practices that are infused with meaning by the biblical narrative and the community's experience of life, bringing about transformed individuals and communities, creating a different identity. Such transformation (making disciples by teaching them Christ's ways, is the sole purpose for the existence of the church) is achieved by people participating and excelling in these practices.[38] Yet a caution is equally important: as powers, these practices have the potential to fall, producing results

35. McClendon, *Ethics,* 2nd ed., 179.
36. Ibid., 180.
37. Ibid., 181.
38. McClendon, "Practice of Community Formation," 94.

contrary to what was expected. Therefore, the understanding of the church as a cluster of powerful practices should be a necessary and helpful point in the theological task of interpreting the realities of the church, not only understanding its strengths, but also seeing its weaknesses and challenges. After all, "Not every 'church' is a front of Christian practice and faith, nor is every liturgy life-breathing though it be called Lord's Supper or Eucharist most holy."[39] Consequently, the church must continuously reevaluate and reexamine its practices, being open to "have their understanding of the story constantly challenged by what others have discovered in their attempt to live faithful to that tradition,"[40] hence it is an invitation to an open dialogue and a reminder for pastors to allow different voices, even critical ones, to be heard and reviewed in a loving and caring community.

Preaching as a Powerful Practice

What is the place of preaching in this reflection on practices and power? First of all, preaching is a practice that helps to shape the lives of individual Christians and of communities of believers. In his extensive work on powers and preaching, Campbell argues,

> The act of preaching plays a central role in the church's interpretive performance of Scripture. In this role, preaching embodies an essential, distinctive performance of the story of Jesus. Specifically, preaching enacts a concrete ethical performance of Jesus' third way—the way of active, nonviolent resistance to and engagement with the principalities and powers of the world. The preaching of the church re-enacts this ethical option at the heart of the story of Jesus.[41]

Thus Campbell highlights the complex reality that preaching and preachers find themselves in. Using the example of ethics of nonviolent resistance, he argues that it is nearly impossible for the practice of preaching to live up to that ethic. Very often the pulpit itself often becomes the place of dominance and violent oppression:

---

39. An extensive analysis of the Lord's Supper as a powerful practice can be found in McClendon, "Practice of Community Formation," 91–94. Also Yoder, *Body Politics*, 14–27.
40. Hauerwas, *Community of Character*, 93.
41. Campbell, *Word Before the Powers*, 79–80.

> The purpose of the sermon becomes that of winning a victory over the people in the pews. The preacher places himself or herself above the congregation and employs manipulation or threats in order to coerce people toward a certain position. Rather than helping to set people free from captivity to the powers of the Domination System, the preacher simply reinforces that system in the relationship between preacher and parishioner.[42]

While Campbell emphasizes the potential dangers of how preaching can be used, he maintains a positive view of it, arguing that it is the practitioner (their church, or denomination) that is in danger of turning preaching into a dangerous tool of violence and domination. Nevertheless, whilst continuous theological and spiritual development of a preacher, as well as appropriate denominational structures ensuring accountability of its leaders, is important, I would argue that preaching, being a practice, has the ability to claim its ultimate importance in the eyes of the practitioners (no matter how good the style or content of preaching can be), causing damage to the community of faith.

In Russian Baptist communities, preaching as a practice has intentional participants—preachers and listeners, and, of course, God. It has developed standards of excellence, which, first of all, is the deep spirituality of a preacher. Preaching has clearly identified goods internal—listening to the word of God produces faith, a virtue that enables individual Christians to follow the Way of Christ. At the same time, through my analysis of the ministry of proclamation, I have shown that preaching influences churches in more ways than producing faith in listeners—its traditionally assumed outcome. Various contributing factors need to be considered here. First is the way preaching is understood: in the Russian context it is seen as almost exclusively a result of God's involvement with a preacher. Hence, a reverent and submissive attitude to both the messenger and his message is expected and even enforced by the church leadership. Second, the participants; is this ministry open to all gifted members of the congregation? Or is it for pastors only? In most cases, preaching is limited to male members approved by the pastor and the church council. Such exclusiveness conveys an important message to the rest of the flock: the task of biblical interpretation is the prerogative of people with special anointing from the Spirit. Therefore, whilst the Bible is fairly widely read in Baptist circles, few people go beyond the

---

42. Ibid., 84.

surface, literal understanding of the text, and the majority find it hard to apply the message to their lives.

Third is the preacher's privileged position. In Russian churches, preachers are not treated as ordinary members, accountable to the general assembly. Instead, they form the spiritual elite of a church. Often they are literally positioned above the congregation, being provided a platform to sit on during worship services, with pulpits being elevated even further. In addition to such visible signs of recognition, preachers (particularly the leaders of local churches) and their families are treated differently, especially in the way church discipline is applied to them in a lot more relaxed fashion.[43] Furthermore, as preachers are seen as "God's anointed," and thus unable to err, any criticism toward their personalities or ministry is seen as dangerous activity, which can bring serious retributions from God.

Fourth is the listeners, who, unfortunately, are rarely encouraged to reflect and engage critically with the message from the pulpit. Instead, they are told to listen and absorb the sermon as the incontestable truth of God This brings significant consequences for the development of Russia's Baptists—the perception of preaching, as the central and the most important practice of the church, and its practitioners, as people with special anointing and authority, has resulted in pulpits becoming attributors of power, effectively alienating Christians from involvement in individual in-depth Bible study, and creating two categories of church members—lay and clergy.[44] Now, if the cornerstone of Baptist identity is understood in the form of a hermeneutical vision as suggested by McClendon, which implies the necessity for individual and congregational involvement with the biblical text, then it is possible to speak of the destructive power of preaching as a force that removes the Bible from people's lives, leaving it in the hands of a few carefully selected practitioners.

The primary danger of preaching is that it can suppress communal reading of the Scripture, substituting it with the pastor's message (no matter how good and polished it might be), thus separating the story from the community of faith. Preaching may teach doctrines, but they remain as disjointed moral or religious utterances, or even worse, slogans that people proclaim but rarely believe and follow. Hence, preaching becomes deformative for

43. E.g. Popov, "Evangelical Christians-Baptists," 259–60.

44. Popov notes that various publications in the *BV* were targeting different audiences. Devotional readings, for example, were viewed as appropriate for any audience. However the term "Bible studies" was used in relation to materials for "professional ministers," and considered unfit for ordinary Christians ("Evangelical Christians-Baptists," 258).

the baptistic identity as it removes the major mark, the core conviction that constitutes the identity of the group. This raises an important question of safeguarding: How can a church keep herself right, addressing her own weaknesses and imperfections, even in such an integral practice for her worship as preaching? This will be the subject of the next chapter.

Conclusion

What then is the conclusion? Practices constitute the life of the church; they possess formative powers, which help to preserve and transmit Christian identity. However, practices have the potential to rebel against the reign of the Lamb through their tendency to claim ultimate importance in the eyes of their practitioners. Thus, every practice must be seen as a powerful practice with both formative and destructive potential, with ability to produce virtues, but also result in vices.

The concept of power becomes particularly challenging, since churches often see themselves as immune to such temptations. Yet the neglect may cause serious consequences, when various practices of the believing community turn into the fallen powers which are in conflict with the risen Christ. Preaching is one of those powerful practices—often perceived as the most important instrument in forming disciples of Baptist churches. Nonetheless, the way this tool is used frequently results in the separation of listeners from the sacred story that it claims to bring to life.

8

Reading the Bible in Community

Introduction

CHAPTER 7 HIGHLIGHTED THE destructive potential of the practice of preaching, which unfortunately is often neglected. This conclusion defines my next step. I am going to address a question: What kind of preaching is required to preserve and develop its constructive and formative powers, whilst being aware of the possible damaging effects? Since preaching cannot be separated from either the Bible or a local church, the starting point must be communal hermeneutics—how the Bible is read in a community of believers.

Baptists see the Bible as authoritative Scripture, and not a mere piece of antique textual material, hence their reading strategies may differ from those employed in academia. The church reads biblical text seeking its literal and spiritual senses, using such approaches as typological reading. The existing safeguarding strategy against potential misinterpretations is reading the Scripture in a community of saints, being guided by the Holy Spirit. The results of their interpretive activities must be projected onto their moral living, providing necessary validation of the meaning of the text. To make such reading possible, the church has to be a community, where people with different levels of theological and biblical literacy are actively involved at various levels of interpretation.

It might be necessary to set some limits to this reflection on baptistic hermeneutics, considering the complexity and even controversy of the subject. I recognize the existing diversity of convictions in Baptist congregations regarding biblical inspiration, the role of the Holy Spirit in the process of interpretation, and authority in interpreting the sacred text that individuals within these churches may hold. Due to the limitations of this work, I chose to ignore those differences. In addition, this chapter must not be seen as prescriptive for churches. Rather it is a theological justification for my claim that reading the Bible in a community of faith (which includes the practice of preaching, existing within a wider cluster of practices of reading the Bible) serves as an important safeguarding strategy against the destructive potential of the powerful practice of preaching. Therefore, in the next step I will turn to the practice of reading the Bible. Its understanding is of particular importance here because although, as with any practice, it possesses destructive potential, it also "contains its own corrective."[1] This self-corrective potential of the practice will be addressed next: How does the church read the book, which holds instructions for its life and serves as a guardian against potential abuses caused by other practices?

The Question of Communal Hermeneutics

In Russia there is a saying, "*Chitai kak napisano*," which means "read as it is written." When used in relation to biblical interpretation, the phrase implies that reading and understanding the Bible is not hard—all one needs to understand the book is to be literate. Russians are far from being unique in such an approach to the Scripture. Consider Randy Hatchett's reference to the literalism present in baptistic communities all over the world,

> Baptists have not produced many theologians . . . They addressed pastoral problems in the contexts of believing churches who sought concrete obedience to their living and present Lord. Yet we should marvel at the quality (and quantity) of their work, even though they naively read the text as an immediate expression of God's will and failed to account adequately for historical distance between themselves and the text.[2]

This may be a good starting point for my exploration of baptistic hermeneutics.[3] Now, whereas I hope that this chapter will be of practical use for churches in Russia, I am not attempting to exhaust the subject of

---

1. McClendon, *Doctrine*, 35.
2. Hatchett, "Hermeneutics of Conversion," 37.
3. For further reading on this subject see Birch, "Baptists and Biblical Interpretation," 153–71, and Parushev, "Baptistic Convictional Hermeneutics," 172–90.

hermeneutics in Baptist communities in the few following pages. This is an attempt to place the practice of preaching within a context of communal hermeneutics, consequently highlighting the existing unbalanced approach to proclamation, which is damaging to the witness of the church.

Andrey Puzynin argues that throughout their history Russian baptists were similar to other evangelicals in their approach to biblical hermeneutics, which was "characterized by Christocentrism, intratextuality, literal and figurative interpretation, interpretive pluralism, and the governing role of the Apostles' Creed."[4] However, various Western missionaries and teachers who came to post-Soviet countries after the fall of the Iron Curtain have rejected previously used methods as unscientific, and instead have introduced new approaches to biblical interpretation (particularly the inductive Bible study method).[5] These methods were introduced as scientific and objective in discerning the meaning of the text through author's intent, and hence were perceived as able to bring much desired theological unity into the diverse baptistic ranks. Nevertheless, Puzynin claims that such an approach fails at various levels, since, first, it does not account for existing traditions, thus creating "a chasm between traditional communities of faith and newly-created educational institutions."[6] Second, it does not allow for alternative thinking, effectively condemning everyone who does not follow the same rules. Third, it discourages a community's involvement in the process of interpretation, emphasizing the role of the experts and thus diminishing the role of people without special training. Finally, it paves the way to use biblical interpretation "as a powerful tool for the ideological support of hierarchical structures . . . for absolutizing their views on certain theological or practical issues."[7]

Instead Puzynin develops a paradigm of differential-integral hermeneutics in his call to reconstruct context-based practices of biblical interpretation. He starts with A. K. M. Adam, offering a critique of hermeneutical methods that insist on the existence of a single meaning of biblical text. Adam argues that instead of searching the meaning in the text, one has to turn to the readers, since meaning emerges as they

---

4. Puzynin, "Tradition of the Gospel Christians," 50.

5. The contemporary state of Russian Baptist biblical interpretation and the existing discrepancies between modern approaches to interpretation prevailing in theological schools and more traditional views predominantly held in churches are addressed in Bokova, "Bibleiskaia ekzegetika i germenevtika," 216–26.

6. Puzynin, "Tradition of the Gospel Christians," 40.

7. Ibid., 40–41.

work towards shared understanding.[8] Based on the claim that prior to the emergence of critical scholarship there existed plurality in interpretation, which nonetheless did not result in interpretive chaos, Adam notes that "critical scholarship did not usher in the era of stable, scientifically certain interpretation."[9] Thus, interpretive focus shifts "from the discovery of the one and only correct meaning that subsists in a text to the interpreting human subjects and communities."[10]

Despite the value of Adam's views, particularly in emphasizing the role of an interpretative community, several deficiencies in his approach were highlighted by Vanhoozer. The first is the possibility of misrepresenting God, Jesus, and the gospel because of the "plurality of interpretations."[11] Adam's approach does not address the necessity of safeguarding against intentional misinterpretation. The second problem follows, which is an insistence on extreme subjectivity of interpretation, and its reliance on social structures, since, as noted by Adam,

> interpretation is a necessarily subjective, value-laden activity. The text, while possibly existing as an objective set of data, cannot function in interpretation to authorize or rule out given readings apart from the set of interests and presuppositions that interpreters bring to their endeavors. The work of interpretation is not so much methodological as conventional.[12]

Vanhoozer attempts to deal with the question of plurality of interpretation without turning interpretation into something infinite and arbitrary. He sets his task to "affirm the fruitfulness and goodness of textual and interpretive polyphony without discrediting the integrity and specificity of the canonical witness to Jesus Christ."[13] Thus, his approach becomes a corrective to Adam's subjectivity by insistence on studying the text in its historical context (including linguistic conventions and historically appropriated interpretations), whilst allowing the diversity of interpretive methods, which are contextually bound.[14] Still, Vanhoozer's main

---

8. Adam, *Faithful Interpretation*, 5.
9. Ibid., 52.
10. Puzynin, "Tradition of the Gospel Christians," 42.
11. Vanhoozer, "Four Theological Faces," 139.
12. Adam, *Faithful Interpretation*, 130.
13. Vanhoozer, "Four Theological Faces," 133.
14. Ibid., 141.

emphasis remains on original authorial intent, since the Scripture is first of all the word of God.[15]

Puzynin identifies several limitations of Vanhoozer's method. First, the impossibility to access biblical writers and their original context, which creates serious challenges in defining original authorial intent.[16] Second, the erroneous understanding that readers cannot contribute to the meaning of the text, only being able to discover shades of authorial intention. According to Vanhoozer, "The reader is not the begetter of meaning but rather a wet nurse who nurtures a discourse not of her own making. The text is a child of authorial discourse yet, precisely as begotten by authors, it can grow."[17] Puzynin rightly points out that such understanding does not leave space for various facets of meaning, which are "creatively constructed under the guidance of the Holy Spirit (or without it)."[18] Furthermore, Vanhoozer's approach does not resolve the problem of conflicting understandings of authorial intent. And finally, one of its main weaknesses is that it leaves little to no part for a Christian community to play in the process of interpretation. Puzynin argues that this

> approach seems to assume. . . that Christian communities cannot interpret Scripture correctly and wisely if they do not have trained scholars with the requisite skills and knowledge for the retrieval of original meanings. However, it was demonstrated that the tradition of the Gospel Christians was developed even behind the Iron Curtain, on the assumption that God is the true author of the Russian Synodal translation of the Bible completed in 1876. Despite their lack of professional training, their readings and literal/figurative interpretations had the power to nourish and transform lives in a totalitarian and hostile milieu.[19]

Thus Puzynin turns to Pol Vandevelde for an approach that could serve as a middle ground and compensate for the shortcomings of Adam's and Vanhoozer's opposing methods. Vandevelde argues that the art of interpretation is not a dichotomy based on the necessary choice between monism and pluralism as conflicting interpretative methods. Instead, he develops a notion of purposeful interpretation, which attributes an important role to

15. Puzynin, "Tradition of the Gospel Christians," 44.
16. Ibid., 45.
17. Vanhoozer, "Four Theological Faces," 141.
18. Puzynin, "Tradition of the Gospel Christians," 45.
19. Ibid., 45.

a community, as well as a text since "interpretive communities come to a text with their strategies of reading, and the text serves as an occasion for those strategies to play out."[20] Vandevelde suggests that the chasm between monism and pluralism should be viewed not as a conflict, but rather "two theoretical positions on two different aspects of interpretation." Consequently, he introduces the concepts of "event" and "act" as a way of defining the two approaches, and bringing them together as different facets of one process of interpretation:

> By event I mean the fact that we as speakers and interpreters participate in a culture and a language that carry with them concepts, values, and habits of which we might not be aware, so that our interpretation is also something taking place in a tradition. By act, I mean an act of consciousness: someone interpreting a text makes a statement or an utterance and through his or her act is committed regarding the truth of what is said, his or her truthfulness, and the rightness or appropriateness of what is said, so that, if prompted, the interpreter must be ready to defend the interpretation made regarding these three claims.[21]

Vandevelde refers to three levels of meaning present in a process of interpretation, with interpreters normally focusing either on all three (in such case the suggested levels represent "an ascending order" in which interpretation happens). These levels are the author's intention, the literal meaning of the text, and the representative content of the text, which is "the meaning that readers see."[22] Understanding the literal meaning of the text depends on the interpreter's language abilities, and authorial intent. Since the latter, whilst being clear in most cases, cannot be unquestionably defined due to the impossibility of meeting the original author and recreating the original context, all these categories of meaning have to be in continuous interaction.[23]

Such supposition brings an important conclusion—it is the process of interpretation, rather than any of the abovementioned levels of meaning, which yields constancy to an interpretation. Both the interpreter and

---

20. Vandevelde, *Task of the Interpreter*, 2.

21. Ibid., 3–4.

22. Ibid., 8–9. Frei sees literal meaning as something that is defined by the consensus of the reading community. Thus, it should not be seen as something static, but dynamic, allowing transformation and development (*Types of Christian Theology*, 15).

23. Vandevelde, *Task of the Interpreter*, 11.

the receiving community are given significant roles in that process. The interpreters must prove the truth of their interpretive claims at every level of interpretation, as well as make a case for the correctness of their interpretation and its relevance to their context depending on the purpose of the interpretation—"to reinforce such a situation or challenge it."[24] Subsequently, this establishes the need for the interpreter to be accountable to the community, which can accept or reject suggested meaning. Hence, interpreters must see themselves as part of "the community of investigators," functioning as interdependent partners.[25] Therefore, sound scriptural interpretation should encompass all the abovementioned levels of interpretation; it should attempt to address the author's intent in writing the text, provide semantic analysis, and present the representative content, enabling the readers to see their story reflected in the biblical narrative.

With this evaluation of the role of a community in interpretation, it might be helpful to turn to Stephen E. Fowl and L. Gregory Jones who, whilst arguing that it is impossible to discover a context-independent method for reading the Scripture, reject anarchy or subjectivism as an arbiter in understanding the Bible. The context in which the community of believers finds itself, contributes to the way the Bible is read and interpreted. Besides, it is through reading in the community that the meaning can be discerned, and only when the communities' lives embody their scriptural interpretation.[26] The need to live out the interpreted biblical text highlights an important notion of Christian attitude to the Bible as containing a narrative which is normative for their lives. That brings an extra dimension into the process of interpretation, which becomes more than mere textual interpretation, but interpretation of the Holy Scripture guided by the Holy Spirit. According to Vandevelde,

> as a text the Bible can be read in many different ways and with many different goals. Christians however, do not read the Bible just as a document, as nonbelievers do, but as a revelation . . . The meaning of words, which is carried by the letter and is thus a literal meaning, is determined by human convention . . . By contrast, the meaning of the things (res), carrying the divine intention, is the spiritual meaning. Accordingly, Christian biblical interpreters agree that, besides the literal meaning, there is a spiritual sense in

---

24. Ibid., 104.
25. Ibid., 104.
26. Fowl and Jones, *Reading in Communion*, 20–21.

the Bible that we can uncover by paying special attention to the text under the guidance of the Spirit.[27]

The pursuit of this spiritual sense is something that has been helping Christians across the world grow deeper in their understanding of faith and enabling them to persevere in their witness, regardless of the often hostile environment. For in spite of the progress and wider accessibility of theological education, the majority of baptistic churches are being planted, living, and growing under the lead (or even devoid of any formal leadership) of people without formal theological training. The only training they receive is through reading and discussing the Bible in their communities, which does not expose them to any of the modern theories of biblical interpretation.[28] And it is both literal meaning and a spiritual sense of the biblical text discovered within the community of believers that continues to inspire and motivate people to walk the Way of Christ.[29]

Obviously, this pattern of reading would be incomplete without the means by which the readers moved from the literal to the spiritual sense. McClendon notes that the means that serve as bridges binding spiritual and literal senses of the Scripture are the types through which a typological reading of the Bible works (which, nevertheless, is not an argument in favor of the metaphorical reading).[30] Finally, such reading happens according to a number of rules. First is "Christological: What Scripture ascribes to Je-

---

27. Vandevelde, *Task of the Interpreter*, 127.

28. This is not an attempt to diminish the value of the developments in the field of biblical studies, but a call to develop various critical skills within a Christian community, enabling its members to discern wisely how the Scripture could be applied to their lives. Thus, this approach is not an alternative to more scholarly views of the process of interpretation, but is another facet of a complex subject of biblical hermeneutics.

29. McClendon, *Doctrine*, 36. Cf. Fish similarly argues that communal interpretation serves as a safeguard against subjectivism in interpretation, and leads to the meaning of the text being rather determinate (Fish, *Doing what Comes Naturally*, 138). Responding to the worry of subjectivism in communal interpretation, and thus, addressing the problem of the "hermeneutical circle," McClendon argues that this problem comes as modernity's "yearning for foundational (and yet nontheological!) truth," which presumably could have been resolved if "we (Christians) periodically disown our Book, disclaim our intimate connection with it, and attempt to read it as though it were indeed something from an alien world. But apart from the historical detour to be reported next, the alienation was a false one." Instead, he suggests that the problem of the hermeneutical circle when speaking about the Bible, and the church reading it, is similar to the problem of the hermeneutical circle "belonging to the letters exchanged between a pair of lovers." Thus, he argues that the problem does not exist.(McClendon, *Doctrine*, 39).

30. McClendon, *Doctrine*, 37; Frei, *Eclipse of Biblical Narrative*, 2–3.

sus must not be denied by the reading of (other) Scripture." The second is based upon the unity of the Bible, insisting that "'No Christian reading may deny either the unity of Old and New Testaments or the congruence ... of that unity with the ascriptive literalism" asserted in the first rule. The third rule allows readings which are not in contradiction with either rule one or two.[31] Thus McClendon argues,

> The baptist vision is the way the Bible is read by those who (1) accept the plain sense of Scripture as its dominant sense and recognize their continuity with the story it tells, and who (2) acknowledge that finding the point of that story leads them to its application, and who also (3) see past and present and future linked by a "this is that" and "then is now" vision, a trope of mystical identity binding the story now to the story then, and the story then and now to God's future yet to come.[32]

The notion of discernment of the spiritual sense and the posture of the interpreters towards the text they use as containing a normative story for their lives raises the need of "validation of meaning."[33] This means that the end product of the process of interpretation, which is the meaning that addresses relevant situations in which the interpretive community finds itself, the meaning that has power to reinforce such situations, or challenge them, must be approved and accepted by the community.[34] Hence, the whole process of interpretation shifts from being the task of the educated few, as assumed by Vanhoozer, to the community of believers, inevitably losing ground for claims of scientific precision, being prone to diverse voices and opinions.[35] Thus, Puzynin notes,

> The process of validation is dialogical, openended, and provisional. The community will need to adjust its interpretations of scripture and of the external world in light of their contingent experiences, as well as of internal and cultural crises that require ongoing hermeneutical activity.[36]

---

31. McClendon, *Doctrine*, 37–38.
32. Ibid., 45.
33. Puzynin, "Tradition of the Gospel Christians," 49–50.
34. Vandevelde, *Task of the Interpreter*, 104.
35. Fowl and Jones, "Scripture, Exegesis, and Discernment," 113.
36. Puzynin, "Tradition of the Gospel Christians," 50.

There are two consequences of such an approach to the interpretation. First, it allows space for members of the community with various levels of knowledge to be involved in an ongoing process of interpreting their sacred book, and thus interpretation becomes inclusive rather than exclusive practice.[37] Furthermore, such an approach does not only allow communal participation, but requires a community to be present,[38] since its members serve as co-interpreters as well as practitioners, and therefore validators of the product of the interpretation. Consequently, the Bible, in order to remain the transforming and redemptive word of God for the people of God, must be read within the community of disciples, who are actively engaged in discerning its meaning and living it out under the guidance of the Holy Spirit.

Practices of Reading the Bible

Addressing the subject of communal hermeneutics, the first question that has to be answered is who are the participants of the process of scriptural interpretation? According to McClendon there are only two—"the narrator and the hearers"—with God being the narrator. The hearers, therefore, must be all the readers of the Bible. Such understanding allows the Bible to become the Holy Scripture, normative for our lives. Furthermore, since no one can claim the position of the narrator, the reading of the Bible remains a communal exercise, a solution to potential intentional and unintentional misinterpretations. The Bible becomes the book that challenges the convictions of its readers, asks uncomfortable questions, and sets the course for the ongoing transformation of the believers' lives.[39]

The importance of reading the Scripture in the church does not presuppose that mere pronouncing of the words written on its pages (the process of reading itself) triggers some magical sequence of events. Whilst this might seem like common sense, it should not be taken for granted that reading the Bible in the community takes place in every church. Far too often, church activities which constitute reading of the Bible, such as preaching and small group Bible study, instead contribute to its gradual removal from the church's life and practice. In chapter 5, I have referred to the damage that preachers' authority produces in Russian Baptist churches,

---

37. Ibid., 51.
38. McClendon, "New Way to Read the Bible," 266–67.
39. McClendon, *Doctrine*, 40–41.

usurping the right of the congregation to read and interpret biblical truth. Similarly, small group Bible studies often limit the circle of the interpretive interests of its participants to the discovery of what a particular text means by asking a simple question: "Is everything clear? Do you have questions?" (and in rare cases by addressing some commentaries of the Bible). Unfortunately, the frequent response to the first question is "yes," and the second is "no," with people assuming they understand the story because it sounds familiar, or out of fear of revealing their ignorance, thus choosing not to engage in discussion.

When teaching does not go beyond ensuring a superficial understanding of words and sentences that constitute the biblical narrative, the transformative power of the biblical text is severely restricted, if not annulled. In addition, the use of the Russian Baptist "traditional" approach to interpretation leads to the Bible being read via numerous references to other biblical passages, at best helping people to memorize biblical bites, whilst often leading to listeners' inability to cohere Biblical narrative with their life story. Frequent intolerance to any interpretation which differs from the developed traditional understanding of various scriptural texts is another persistent problem.[40] Such hermeneutical conservatism not only rejects new ways and approaches to interpretation, but more importantly labels them as heretical and sinful, thus making communal reading—which permits various voices to be heard in an open dialogue—practically impossible.

I must pause now to reemphasize the point I have already made: this work is neither an attack on interpretive strategies of Russian Baptists, nor a call to redesign their preaching style by introducing more sound or more popular Western alternatives. While I believe self-criticism is important for Baptists in Russia to learn, it must be noted that there are no perfect preaching styles, just like there are no perfect churches. Weaknesses can be found in any approach to preaching, whether traditional or modern.

I believe the main issue that is at stake here is inadequacy of any approach to preaching *as the main or often the only way of introducing the Scripture* into the community of faith. No approach or style of preaching can address a variety of issues related to communal interpretation of the Bible

---

40. For a critique of such traditional reading of biblical texts and churches' unwillingness to accept new approaches to interpretation, see Antonenko, "Principles for Interpreting Jesus' Parables."

and its projection onto the communal life, thus it can be easily criticized as reductionist.[41] Hence, a clear understanding that any preaching must be seen as only a limited facet in a complex subject of communal hermeneutics might be a reconciling solution and a way forward. An open Bible does not inevitably turn a group of people, gathered around it, into a community of interpreters. Neither does listening to a great amount of preaching turn its listeners into experienced readers and interpreters of the word.

Therefore, Baptist communities must make a conscious effort in transforming the focus of their engagement with the Scripture, from mere (and inevitably shallow) listening to deeply self-involving ongoing transformative experience. The church needs to develop the ranks of often complacent listeners into communities of interpreters, whose voices will be able to provide the much needed challenge of the "predispositions, ideologies, and theological presumptions" with which people approach the Bible.[42] Some will have to become biblical scholars, highlighting the need for churches to partner with theological educational institutions. The process of "developing people skilled in the application of critical biblical scholarship"[43] defines the necessity of providing such opportunity for them by relieving these people from other duties. Hence, church congregations need to take responsibility for identifying, educating, and using their members for the ministry of biblical interpretation. The would-be scholars should be aware of their duty to serve their church families with humility and respect. And finally, theological schools must see the need to cooperate with communities of faith, responding to their needs and listening to their concerns.[44]

Theological education plays a significant role in stimulating deeper engagement with the Bible. Nonetheless, it would be wrong to assume that the

---

41. For an extensive critique of expository preaching and preaching as teaching see Brown, *Transformational Preaching*, chs. 1–2. Alternatively, Campbell offers a critique of narrative preaching, arguing that the danger and limitations of this approach is that "human experience becomes the focus of the sermon, rather than God in Jesus Christ, whose identity is rendered in the biblical narrative" (*Preaching Jesus*, 141). Campbell nevertheless falls into a similar trap of pursuing a perfect preaching method. Although he recognizes the limitations of preaching, and the danger for the corrupt practices of the community of faith to have the power to corrupt the practice of rhetoric, he still sees proclamation as the main instrument of resisting the fallen powers (*Word Before the Powers*, 140–41). Thus, he attempts to offer a corrective to the narrative preaching by developing his alternative approach.

42. Fowl and Jones, "Scripture, Exegesis, and Discernment," 124.

43. Ibid., 125.

44. Ibid., 125–26.

sole purpose of this book is to increase the number of theology students. The Holy Spirit gives churches different gifts, and not everyone is called to full-time ministry in the field of biblical studies. However, this is not an excuse for the majority of churchgoers to pass their responsibility of becoming interpreters of the word onto their pastors and other trained ministers. Rather, it is a call to start thinking creatively about how the Bible can be brought into the life of every Christian, how the narratives that we find in the Scripture can turn into the life stories of the church members.

Such an objective, to develop a church into a community of interpreters, may seem a scary proposition for some leaders, since it involves risking losing control over various matters of congregational life.[45] Here it might be helpful to refer to Sharon D. Welch's concept of ethics of risk, instead of ethics of control,[46] where "ethical actions are not primarily those that control outcomes," since they equip communities and individuals for ongoing growth and development.[47] Obviously, I am not comparing Russian Baptist churches to oppressed groups that need liberation, which is the focus of Welch's work; however, the process of transforming passive listeners into the community of interpreters requires a sequence of steps, which may bring unexpected results. In addition, regardless of the challenges posed by such an unpredictable and open-ended venture, stimulating individual and communal engagement with the Scripture is a necessary work of allowing the Holy Spirit to play a greater role in the lives of the church members.

Studying the Bible in small groups, creating opportunities for lay members to be involved in preaching and teaching, various other activities that both make people interested in reading the Scripture, and engage them in sharing their insights on how the text speaks into their lives—the list of such practices can go on. Yet, since the focus of this study is not to prescribe a solution but to stimulate further reflection, I am not going to stipulate

---

45. A few years ago I attended a members meeting at a large Baptist church in Russia, where the congregation had "appointed" the church council. During that process, the church members were given a list of names, drafted by the pastor and few other members of the existing council, for their approval. I asked why the congregation was not trusted with nominating potential candidates, to make the election a communal experience guided by the Holy Spirit. The pastor honestly answered, "If we do that, they (the members of the church) will certainly vote brother Victor and brother Alexander in, which we (the pastor and the existing council) do not want."

46. Welch, *Feminist Ethics of Risk*.

47. Campbell develops a notion of ethics of risk in relation to the subject of integrity of preaching, which he presents as an instrument of bringing the message of peace and nonviolent action into the church (*Word Before the Powers*, 89–90).

an expanded list of steps or practices that churches have to introduce into their ministry. This is a process that every congregation needs to go through depending on its context and resources. At this stage, it would suffice to say that there are no quick fixes or instant solutions, or one-size-fits-all strategies of turning a church into a community of biblical interpreters. However, the process of searching and trying various methods, of discerning individual and communal gifts, and listening to God's newly discovered voice, is rewarding by itself, both for the whole congregation and its leader(s).

Conclusion

The focus of this chapter was on practices of reading the Bible in the community. I have argued that the interpretive strategy adopted by Baptists was based on their understanding of two senses of biblical text: literal and spiritual. The understanding of literal meaning as dependent on the changing realities of the life of the community, and spiritual meaning, discovered by typological reading of the text, presupposes the need for the existence of the community of interpreters who can both discover the meaning but also offer its necessary validation by implementing it in their lives.

The need for the existence of such a community (serving as a safeguarding strategy against the potential destructive forces of its practices) leads to the necessary existence of a number of practices of reading the Bible in community. I have argued that Baptist churches must become intentional about developing their members into biblical interpreters. First of all, this emphasizes the need for cooperation between churches and theological schools. However, the process of raising biblical interpreters must not end with biblical scholars, who have graduated with qualifications in theology. Every member of the Christian community needs to be involved in the process of hermeneutics. This leads me to the final stage of this work—focusing on preaching as one of the key practices of reading the Bible in the community.

9

Preaching, Church, and University

Introduction

AT THE CONCLUSION OF a lengthy research project on the subject of Baptist preaching in Russia, one may be tempted to offer a solution in the form of a preaching manual that could be shared among pastors and lay preachers, aiming at solving Russia's various preaching ills. Having listened to long and often uninspiring (to say the least!) sermons, having spoken with different people about their impressions of preaching, and, having seen numerous problems that arise in churches as a result of the failure of their pulpit ministry, writing a denouncing pamphlet claiming that the current practice has to be drastically reformed may sound like an attractive idea. However, I would like to focus on something good and precious that Russian Baptist churches have preserved, and which, with due critical reflection and modification, can become a starting point for a much-needed transformation and renewal, not only of the practice of proclamation, but of the whole Russian Baptist movement.

What I am going to write next might surprise quite a few people. Moreover, some of the people that personally know me and my views on preaching would probably be stunned, just like I am amazed myself. The good and precious element, which I believe can serve as a cornerstone for the future transformation of Baptist preaching practices and lead to reinforcement or, more precisely, rediscovery of their ecclesial identity, is the phenomenon of multiple preaching that is common in a Russian Baptist worship service. However, let me say a word of self-justification before I hear an astounding "What on earth is he talking about?" from the western readers used to a one-hour service with a fairly short sermon, and my Russian sisters and brothers, who suffer (and I am not hesitant to use this rather strong word) week in and week out, enduring numerous exhortations on themes vastly removed not only from people's daily lives, but from anything real, during their two-to-three-hour-long services.

Three important provisions are to be made before I proceed. First is the purpose of this work. As I have stated earlier, I am not attempting to design a preaching method offering an adaptation of the best homiletical approaches developed in recent years in the Anglo-American Christian context to Russian ecclesial realities. Neither do I aspire to develop and present my own unique homiletical method. Nor is this an effort to argue a case for a revolution in various aspects of Russian Baptists' theology or worship practices. My aim is to offer a starting point for a critical reflection on one of the most important practices that has contributed significantly to the shaping of baptistic churches in Russia and which continues to influence them in various ways. Addressing preaching as one of the practices of reading the Bible in a Christian community, I hope to offer a tool for the furthering of homiletical and hermeneutical thought, first of all, in theological educational institutions.

Second, this work does not approach preaching as a skill that lies in the fields of rhetoric and communication. Hence I do not deal with the question of the preferred homiletical method. These are important issues, however they are not central to this research. I have focused on preaching as, first of all, a social practice. As a practice, preaching may yield diverse results, leading to the development of both virtues and vices. My argument is that in order to nullify its destructive potential, preaching must be practiced within a wider cluster of practices of reading the Bible in the community. Thus, the following discussion will be focused on preaching as a practice of communal hermeneutics.

Third is the important contribution that a concept of baptistic vision brings into the discussion. When the biblical story is understood as a normative narrative that forms both the corporate life of the community of faith and individual lives of its members, it highlights the limitations of preaching. Even the best preaching strategy cannot lead people to appropriate the whole of the biblical story as their story. At best, on its own, preaching can help listeners to adopt certain behavioral patterns, learn a number of doctrines, and serve as a source of motivation and inspiration.

Therefore, what is required is a transformation of the congregation of listeners into a community of interpreters of the word, as there is no other way for the biblical story to penetrate deeply into the lives of people.

In the following pages I will, first of all, address the phenomenon of multiple preaching. However, instead of attributing too much value to its current form, I will argue that Russian Baptist churches need to rediscover the roots of this practice, which was an excellent example of the whole community being involved in the process of discovery and application of the biblical story, of discerning people's spiritual gifts, and of forming their new leaders—a positive lesson from history that can modify the future of their preaching.

Finally, the concluding section of this chapter will raise a question of the relevance of this research. A call to rediscover the communal aspect of biblical interpretation, thus significantly altering churches' takes on preaching, may seem an impossible dream, considering the number of local congregations in Russia (over 1,700), and their cultural and theological diversity. Therefore, first of all, I hope that this book will prompt further discussions, reflections, and research in the areas of Russian Baptist preaching and hermeneutics. This naturally leads me to theological schools, places of ministerial formation, and theological reflection on the practices and convictions of the communities of faith. I will briefly address the controversial nature of the university-church relationships in the Russian context, highlighting the fact that the lack of engagement between ecclesial and educational institutions can be explained through their inability to understand each other's tasks and methods. A brief overview of the curriculums of two major theological schools operating in Russia will reveal the lack of connections between such disciplines as homiletics and Baptist identity. Furthermore, with the subject of identity being almost completely neglected, it raises a question: To what extent does the current educational framework help enhance the understanding of the role and place of preaching—one of the key ecclesial practices—in contemporary Russian Baptist communities and, therefore, what is the role of educational institutions in molding and shaping that identity?

Three Sermons in a Service: Present, Past, and Future

Contemporary Russian Baptist churches are facing numerous problems which they are not always able to identify, willing to admit to, or capable of addressing. Rising Christian nationalism (an oxymoron in itself) among its members is just one of such issues. Recent catastrophic events in the Donetsk and Lugansk regions of Ukraine and the controversial "reunion" of Crimea with Russia sparked huge debates among the ordinary Christians of Russia and Ukraine. Countless discussion threads on social media websites almost inevitably concluded with mutual anathemas and abusive remarks regarding each participant's nationality and stance with God. The tragic absurdity of such a relationship between members of one ecclesial family reveals a significant underlying issue—people's inability to see the existence of a Christian alternative to the current struggles of Russian and Ukrainian political elites. Unfortunately, at the present time, the way of Christ is perceived through the lens of ethnic and political identity, rather than as its viable alternative. The Christian narrative has turned into mere ethical add-ons, being overwhelmed and suppressed by another story, skillfully told through the media.

Does preaching make a difference? Apparently, not much: a lot of contemporary preaching can be described as a crusade against sinful living, which in Russian context means attacking certain social trends, like people's dwindling commitment to church, manifested through their irregular attendance of worship services, as well as some obvious social ills such as divorce, alcoholism, smoking, and others. Such preaching comes with an eschatological warning of Jesus' imminent return and an inevitable threat of judgment and punishment for those who do not comply with the way that has been deemed right and, hence, is propagated by the church and her leaders. To sum up, most preaching either aims at imposing certain ethical restrictions on people's lives or simply cannot be described as any sort of meaningful activity, being a random collection of pious words, biblical quotations, and exhortations.

Popov uses a phrase "the crisis of the genre"[1] addressing the contemporary state of preaching in Russian Baptist churches. He argues that today's preaching can be characterized by the absence of "God's fire that enflames souls," instead offering "dry lections on biblical themes or . . . remote from life's problems talks."[2] While correctly noticing the ongoing crisis, he sees the roots of the problem in churches' attempts to imitate the "western model" of having one sermon, preached exclusively by the pastor, and other "poorly

---

1. Popov, "Otechestvenniaia shkola propovedi v tserkvakh," 44.
2. Ibid., 44.

planned experiments," which eradicated "classical preaching."³ Popov defines "classical preaching" as a tradition of communal preaching, when various "lay members" are involved in this ministry together with the pastor.⁴ The roots of such a practice are seen in a tradition of the Jewish synagogue that was absorbed by the New Testament church. Popov refers to Acts 13:15, which speaks about a synagogue ruler offering Paul and his companions an opportunity to preach an edifying message to the people; also 1 Corinthians 14:26, where the members of the congregation are invited to participate in the ministry of mutual edification.⁵

Whilst it might be easy to disagree with the claim that attempted reforms or western influences have corrupted proclamation in Russia, since such a claim is based solely on the author's subjective opinion, Popov's evaluation of communal preaching might serve as an important stepping stone for this section of my work:

> Democratic approach to the ministry of the Word, rooted in the New Testament, and inherited by Evangelical Christians-Baptists of Russia from their predecessors,⁶ brought significant creative diversity into the worship service, contributing to the emergence of the environment, encouraging the development of the gift of preaching, and brought missionary spirit into the whole congregation.⁷

Omitting the debatable issue of historical succession of the practice of communal preaching, I would like to focus on the positive impact it produced in the first baptistic churches in Russia. Without restating the argument of first three chapters, it might be worth providing a brief summary of what preaching meant for the baptistic movement. First of all, preaching was seen to be a deeply communal exercise, with male and female members involved in this ministry. The lack of ordained pastors defined the absence of established persons of authority in the sphere of biblical interpretation, thus allowing deeper participation of the listeners in the process of interpretation. Moreover, the audience was *encouraged* to share their opinions (including

---

3. Ibid., 44.

4. Ibid., 44.

5. Ibid., 44.

6. Popov argues that various nonconformist movements that appeared in Russia between the twelfth and sixteenth centuries should be seen as "spiritual predecessors" of Baptists. Strigolniks, Molokans, Starovers, Dukhobors, and some others practiced similar open access to preaching ("Otechestvenniaia shkola propovedi v tserkvakh," 37).

7. Popov, "Otechestvenniaia shkola propovedi v tserkvakh, 44.

disagreements) on the proclaimed text. Furthermore, it was the congregational approval, rather than the pastor's sole opinion, that was seen as a necessary element of appointing people for preaching and evangelistic work.

A sense of pursuing something new, of rediscovering the unknown essence of Christian faith, and learning to apply that newly found story to their individual and corporate living, resulted in a formation of a group with a distinct ecclesial identity. These people chose to drastically alter their lives in terms of morals and religious adherence, risking the state-executed persecution for religious dissent, and social alienation, being labeled as bearers of the foreign faith. Unlike preaching in contemporary Baptist churches, that simple communal study of the Bible had a significant impact on the way people built their lives and perceived their identity in the turbulent years of social change of the nineteenth century.

Of course, I am far from idealizing either preaching of the early baptistic communities in Russia or any other aspect of their life and practice. Inevitably, there were conflicts and struggles. Some of them were a direct result of the misuse of Scripture. However, the recognition that no practice is immune to a fall should serve as yet another reminder that the practice of preaching must be placed within a wider cluster of practices of reading the Bible, which includes the development of peoples' critical and analytical skills, by encouraging them to receive quality formal theological and secular education, as well as through the offering of informal educational opportunities through church-based Bible study groups.

To sum up, it is possible to say that the beginning of the Russian Baptist movement was a successful experiment in communal hermeneutics. The practice of *multiple preaching* of primitive baptistic congregations led to the emergence of a clearly defined ecclesial identity, distinct from the dominant Orthodox culture. The absence of rigid traditions, leadership, and worship practices allowed preaching to be a communal practice of discovering the biblical narrative, and of turning that narrative into the life-story of the church.

Whilst a lot of inspiration can be drawn from history, it can hardly be seen as a road map for implementing a full-scale experiment of transforming today's Baptist congregations—marked as they are by the rigidity of their theological convictions and ecclesial practices—into open-minded communities of biblical interpreters. At best, this work can serve as a starting point for a serious discussion on the nature of worship practices and

Preaching in Educational Space

Church and University in Paradox

The contemporary period in the history of theological education in Russia begins in 1989 with the opening of Odessa Theological Seminary. In the first years following the collapse of the USSR, over forty seminaries, institutes, colleges, and Bible schools were opened in Russia, Ukraine, and other former Soviet republics. Mark Elliot points out that nowhere in history did protestant churches have so many programs for full-time theological and ministerial training, as they did in post-Soviet countries.[8] The majority of these institutions were founded, funded, and operated by Christians from the USA.[9] Schools varied from large institutions (within the post-communist context) such as the MTSECB with their own campus, library facilities, and extended faculty, to small one-man organized and taught "seminaries," sometimes run on the premises of local churches.

Addressing the perceived value of theological education, Konstantin Tetereviatnikov notes,

> The essence of the appropriated paradigm was as follows: the evangelical believer, who wanted to become an effective and qualified minister, was supposed to receive appropriate theological training with emphasis on biblical studies, hermeneutics, languages, systematic theology, and applied disciplines, such as homiletics, pastoral ministry, evangelism, discipleship.[10]

At first these schools enjoyed great numbers of students, but many of their graduates did not settle in churches, which did not express substantial interest in supporting educational programs or developing partnerships with schools. Moreover, many local congregations still perceive theological education as damaging to true spirituality, rather than a tool that can assist them in their ministry.

---

8. Elliot, "Bogoslovskoie obrazovaniie v postkommunisticheskii period," 18–19.

9. For a story of the beginning of MTSECB and the role of US Christians in its formation, see Kosinko, "Stanovleniie bogoslovskogo obrazovaniia," 9–13.

10. Tetereviatnikov, "Perspectivi vospitaniia sluzhitelei," 245.

At present, theological education in Russia finds itself in an even more challenging environment. Financial support from foreign sponsors has dwindled. The number of applicants has significantly fallen, either due to the graduates being unable to find employment in churches, or because secular universities with prospects of a more enriching career are winning the battle for prospective students. As a result, many schools and programs have closed. Others are trying to move forward by experimenting with new online and distance-learning courses by developing contextual approaches to Christian learning, and by exploring questions about the kind of graduates they should be preparing in order to address the needs of local churches.

The gap between churches and educational institutions has not been bridged yet. I believe one of the key issues has not been considered in the important ongoing discussion about the future of theological education in Russia. Churches perceive the call to ministry, success in pastoral work, and fruitful preaching to be, first of all, a result of the work of the Holy Spirit. As I noted earlier, any shortcomings or failures in life or ministry are understood as the absence of God's Spirit, due to the wrong condition of the heart of either the preacher or his listeners (or both). Regardless of how educators relate to such an extreme charismatic approach, it is a starting point for most Russian Baptist grass-roots theology and practice.[11] And another important point is this approach to ministry effectively excludes the need for education. It is not surprising therefore, that even today it is

---

11. Employing typologies of contemporary Christianity of Newbigin and Dunn, Parushev develops the concept of the pneumotological stream of contemporary Christianity: "Alongside the two dominant flows of theological thought, there have always been streams of radical and truthful living of the Way of Christ in believing communities committed to the Kingdom vision. They are not much interested in 'What is God like?' or 'How does He operate?' In a child-like fashion they are witnessing God's immediate presence and acts in their lives, using, most of the time sub-consciously, the Socratic language of moral perfection and character formation (or discipleship). God is known by what He does in our midst. By constructing new ways of social living, they succeed in conveying, non-abrasively, the power of God to create the new in those and through those who are united to Christ (2 Cor 5.17). They see themselves embodied in the narrative of the Kingdom of God revealed in and through Christ by the power of the Holy Spirit" (*Christianity in Europe*, 18–19). Without dismissing the value of Christian education, this insight should serve as a reminder of the existence of a viable alternative to the power of reason and theological debate, which was at the heart of the Protestant way of doing church.

not unusual to hear Baptist leaders saying things like, "We do not need theology, since it is already in the Bible."[12]

Nonetheless, many people that are involved in theological education do not account for the existence of such a paradigm[13] or, even worse, dismiss it as senseless and irrelevant. Consider, the following argument by Nicolai Kornilov,

> Our church, our whole brotherhood needs more educated and professional theologians. We have already understood that for ministry in our churches we need more educated ministers. Now we are beginning to think what kind of education we need... We need good, sound, classical theological education. Nobody will contest the fact that a Christian minister is not capable of performing the ministry of the Word, if he does not possess deep knowledge of what the Bible says about God... This knowledge consists of several aspects of theology, such as teaching about God, about Christ—Christology, about humans—biblical anthropology, about Church—ecclesiology. These and other aspects of theology, as well as biblical languages—are important components of education of a serious minister, a good builder of the body of Christ. To be a Christian minister and have no aspirations to develop your thinking and search for answers to everyday spiritual questions, to neglect theological education, is almost the same as when instead of good professional medical treatment people are offered charlatancy.[14]

The unfortunate reality of life for such educators, is that the majority of pastors still do not see a qualification in theology as a must-have for a good minister. Nor do they like being compared to charlatans. This leads to theological education being perceived as damaging to the spirituality of potential ministers, since it is seen as developing pride and the spirit of criticism. Another stance concerning education views seminaries as a threat to existing leaders, since any suggestion that a pastor/preacher needs

---

12. Cherenkov argues that the inability of the church leaders to see the value of theological education is the root of the various problems of contemporary churches (Cherenkov, "Nash baptism," para. 26).

13. Sergienko offers an excellent example of the split between the "old paradigm" of preaching, with a preacher's spirituality seen as the foundation for the successful proclamation of God's word, and the "new approach," where spirituality is replaced with emphasis on hermeneutics, rhetorics, and the lack of exegetical mistakes, which is seen as a key to successful preaching. (Sergienko, "Put k effektivnomu propovedovaniyu," 5–21)

14. Kornilov, "Kakogo roda bogosloviie nam nuzhno?," 10.

to continue learning implies the questioning of their standing with God, their spiritual maturity, which establishes the foundation of their authority, of God's special anointing. Thus it is, first of all, the lack of understanding of what constitutes the identity of Baptist churches that forces the leadership of Baptist communities to hold on to the outer shell of their ecclesial practices, formed through the years of suffering and oppression under the communistic regime, and to reject anything—first of all education—that threatens the cohesiveness of this fragile whole, that in their eyes constitutes the Baptist way of life.

Turning from the church to the university, there is a distinct sense of dissatisfaction and even quiet irritation in the church's perceived inability or, perhaps, unwillingness to accept the "gift of knowledge and enlightenment."[15] The church is seen as a reactionary, conservative institution, "interested in one-way traffic, receiving from education an intellectual image and concrete applied knowledge."[16] At the same time, the university is understood, self-flatteringly, perhaps, to be a place of free thinking and constant pushing of the boundaries of accepted patterns of life and practice. Consequently, there is an assumption that the university's influence on the church is seen as "exclusively negative."[17]

In addition to the lack of understanding mentioned above, educators often perceive their task as developing a theological tradition independent from the church (although insisting that they do it as their service for the church). The university is seen as a place for "non-church theology."[18] All of this contributes to the widening of the gap between ecclesial practice and academic thought. Thus the appearance of Mykhailo Cherenkov's thesis that the church must be blamed for the existing misunderstandings and conflicts can be seen as a result naturally flowing from mutual misunderstanding and, eventually, mistrust. He writes,

> The alienation between the Church and the University continues not because the University is closed or has an antichristian disposition, but because the Church cannot and does not even try to express its faith in forms suitable for the University and to put its faith to an intellectual test in discussions.[19]

15. Cherenkov, "Post-Soviet Protestants," 27.
16. Ibid., 27.
17. Ibid., 26–29.
18. Ibid., 25.
19. Ibid., 28.

While lamenting the failure of the church to reach the level of the university, Cherenkov seems to be interested in developing abstract academic theology.[20] However, in doing so, he misses an important part of the theological task—to discover the convictions of the community of faith, enabling an informed dialogue that can lead to transformation of both dialogue partners. Hence, it is possible to speak of the inevitability of conflict between the church and the university. Each side is acting with their best intentions, and yet is unable to see their inherent and mutually exclusive differences, grounded in dissimilar understandings of spirituality, authority, identity, and purpose.

The Discipline of Homiletics

There are numerous issues that have to be considered in a discussion about the birth, development, and future potential of theological education in Russia. This book neither attempts to resolve nor to identify them all. However, in my study of preaching, and the ways it affects churches through its connection to power, the question of the future of theological education becomes, first of all, a question of developing a particular ecclesial identity, understood not in terms of creedal statements, but in the existence of a binding narrative, able to embrace the diversity of baptistic communities, allowing churches to regain a renewed sense of purpose and unity. Too often the question of identity has been taken for granted, both by the church, with the majority of its members being unable to answer, what makes them Baptists; and seminaries, which, whilst perceiving their task as the formation of Baptist identity and Christian character, did not address the question of what constitutes the identity they were trying to form.[21]

At this stage, it might be helpful to offer a brief overview of the way preaching is taught in two major centers of theological education in Russia: Moscow Theological Seminary of Evangelical Christians-Baptists (MTSECB)—the main educational institution of RUECB—and TCM-International Institute, Austria (TCMII). Whilst TCMII is not Russia-based, I still choose to refer to their preaching program since the institute has a

---

20. Ibid., 30.

21. Sharp addresses these questions, arguing theological education needs to give up the ideas of primacy of individualistic spiritual formation and rediscover the value of discipleship through participation in the life of a Christian community to regain its focus and relevance in Baptist life. ("Kto takiie baptisty segodnia?," 105–6, 123)

major impact on Russian Christian culture through its educational centers in Vladimir, Omsk, and Khabarovsk. Both schools act as important centers of ministerial training, with their M-level studies being an indication of advanced theological research and reflection.

A quick overview of the two courses shows many similarities in the objectives and materials used. TCMII describes their course on homiletics[22] as "a study of the principles of preaching as they relate to rationale, context, content, structure, style, and the delivery of sermons." The rationale of the course is to "help students better communicate the gospel of Jesus Christ in the context of their culture," which is achieved through the analysis of "the principles of preaching."[23] There are several objectives for the course: "Recognize the absolute necessity of maintaining the character of Christ in order to be heard as God's messenger . . . Appreciate the role of preaching in Scripture and in the total scope of ministry . . . Understand and apply the biblical/theological material concerning preaching."[24] The following topics are covered in the progression of studies: the importance of preaching, textual interpretation, structure of sermon, relevance in preaching, how to preach (delivery of sermons), spirituality and intellectual development of preachers, expository preaching, and advanced planning of preaching ministry. The following books are required (all are available in Russian): James Braga, *How to Prepare Bible Messages*; John R. W. Stott, *I Believe in Preaching*; Haddon Robinson, *Biblical Preaching*; Charles H. Spurgeon, *Lectures to My Students*; D. Martyn Lloyd-Jones, *Preaching and Preachers*; Fred B. Craddock, *Preaching*; and Leonid Mikhovich, *Kak Razbit' Skaly? (How to Break the Rock?)*.[25]

The course of MTSECB is described as a "foundational course on the theory and practice of preaching." The rationale of the course is "to lay theoretical foundations and develop practical skills for developing and delivering a sermon."[26] There are several objectives of the course. The students are expected to learn main homiletical concepts, to develop a skill of textual interpretation through studies in exegesis, theology, and homiletics; to de-

---

22. I am referring to one of the two courses on preaching offered by TCMII. The second course, "Advanced Homiletics," is omitted from this overview, as it deals with a more specific subject, "The study and practice of doctrinal preaching." (Mikhovich, syllabus "PT 622 Advanced Homiletics")

23. Mikhovich, syllabus "PT 520 Homiletics."

24. Ibid.

25. Ibid.

26. Sergienko, "Homiletics."

velop skills in formulating a theme of a sermon and developing a sermon outline; to enhance their rhetorical skills; and to develop a better understanding of working with an audience. The course covers three major areas of preaching ministry: preachers' spirituality and calling; the role and the use of biblical text in preaching; and practical steps related to developing and delivering a sermon. The key study materials are Haddon Robinson, *Biblical Preaching* and John R. W. Stott, *The Preacher's Portrait*.[27]

There are three important conclusions to be made from this overview. The first concerns the way preaching is perceived. Both curriculums aim at preparing preachers, who would be able to continue practicing preaching in its traditional way (as a rhetorical instrument that can help to achieve certain goals, whether educational or motivational). No attempt is made to explore the nature of the practice or analyze the existing assumptions regarding the value of preaching, as the central practice of Russian Baptist worship. Secondly, the conclusion relates to the type of materials used in the process of education. The lists of required literature almost exclusively rely on books written by Anglo-American authors. Whilst this is not a suggestion that the use of these sources might be inappropriate or mistaken, it must be recognized that Russian Baptists have developed and continue to exist in a specific cultural context which inevitably affects their perception and practice of preaching, as well as other areas of theology and practice. There are no provisions for such specifics either through studying Russian Orthodox preaching, theology of the Orthodox Church, or through in-depth cultural studies. Finally, the question of Baptist identity, although often raised in recent works of various theologians, who work in the field of Russian and wider post-Soviet baptistic history and ecclesiology, is neglected, being only briefly addressed as part of "the History of the Baptist Movement."

From the example of Russian baptistic history, it is clear that proclamation has developed and evolved together with the church. Various pressures that the church had to cope with affected its preaching. One such change is the shift in the understanding of who can/should be the interpreter of the word. At the early stages of the movement entire congregations were involved in the process of discernment of both the meaning of the biblical text and the appointment of their leaders. Gradually, the pastor became the person with power to make such decisions, and the preaching office was entity which bestowed this power. Therefore, to approach preaching

27. Ibid.

as a mere rhetorical exercise is to miss something very significant for both preachers-in-training and the receiving churches.

From Conflict to Partnership: The Way to Mutual Understanding

Let me offer a brief summary of the argument of this section of my work. An overview of the contemporary relationships between the communities of faith and their educational institutions shows the inevitability of conflict. The existing inability to understand the mutually exclusive cornerstones of their ministries—the supernatural work of God in the church, over against the academic reasoning, research, and critical analysis in the university—results in a clash of paradigms, sometimes leading to a mistaken conclusion that the free-thinking university is rejected by the irrational and reactionary church.

The review of two courses on homiletics, offered by two major theological educational institutions, shows that the way preaching is taught further widens the divide between churches and theological schools. While seminaries teach their students the art of homiletics, which is inseparable from thorough exegesis, and the use of rhetorical devices, churches often perceive these students as people with potentially distorted spirituality, lacking reliance on the Holy Spirit. Furthermore, the existing link between pastoral authority and preaching office, grounded in personal piety and spirituality, effectively excludes a notion of learning to preach in academic settings.

As it stands, the current trend in relationships between baptistic churches and theological schools in Russia does not leave much hope for the future. Their partnership is never equal. Educational institutions fully depend on the support of local churches, which goes beyond financial contributions, but includes churches providing students and helping graduates with employment. As mentioned earlier, the alleged spirit of free thinking and pushing of the boundaries does not meet with much sympathy with the communities of believers. Hence, the existing seminaries, Bible schools, and institutes are forced to adapt to the requirements and demands of the church life or cease to exist.

Nonetheless, despite the present tensions in the relationships between ecclesial and academic institutions, I would like to conclude this project with a positive outlook. I have previously argued that the lack of understanding of mutually self-excluding views on the role of the Holy Spirit and individual learning must be seen as one of the main reasons for the church-university contradictions. Such misunderstandings can be best illustrated through uncomfortable situations that young students of theology often end up in, when they return to their local churches, having participated in a few courses on theological disciplines, thus discovering an alternative reality to the world of a local church. Passionate, unwilling to compromise their newly obtained knowledge, they spark fiery debates with "uneducated" pastors or preachers, trying to enlighten and correct them.

Can such conflicts be avoided in favor of a more pragmatic and mutually respectful position, where the university would not need to give up the free spirit of enquiry, whilst the church would find it easier to involve people from other, less charismatic backgrounds? As previously stated, my aim is not to offer a modified curriculum to resolve existing weaknesses in the way the subject of preaching is approached. At this stage, I would like to suggest only two possible corrections—or better to say, additions—to the existing curriculums.

Firstly, whilst the whole notion of identity is largely a neglected subject for Russian Baptist theological education, it needs to be seen as an important starting point for any studies related to the preparation of preachers. Unless this subject is viewed seriously in educational institutions, all attempts to aid churches in dealing with their problems will be similar to trying to relieve symptoms of the disease without addressing the cause.

The second element relates to the way the question of theology is approached. As McClendon argues,

> Theology is not just "ideas (or words) about God"; it is not a set of changeless beliefs associated with religion; it is not, despite the jokes, erudite discussion of inaccessible nonentities . . . There is a more satisfying notion of what theology is that makes sense to many people: on the one hand, "it represents something deeply self-involving for its adherents"; on the other, even mystical theologies . . . "are attempts systematically to connect mystical experience with what is and is not there in the world—or beyond it."[28]

Such understanding, unlike the previously mentioned idea of the university being a place of nonchurch, pure academic theology, leads to a different relationship between the church, a convictional community, and

---

28. McClendon, *Witness*, 398.

the university, an educational institution which is involved in "systematic study that investigates, interprets, and sometimes re-forms" convictions of a convictional community.[29] This approach presupposes that the university needs the church, which becomes its community of reference, since theology is never neutral, but contextual and self-involving in its character.[30] The systematic study of the convictions of the church, understanding and discovery of what the church really believes in, and how these beliefs were formed, will lead to a greater level of understanding and, subsequently, to greater appreciation of what the church and the university practice and aspire to achieve.

This entire project could be seen as an attempt to implement the above-mentioned suggestions into the study of the practice of proclamation. The answer to the question of the role of preaching in forming, preserving, and passing on the ecclesial identity of Russian Baptists can only be found when preaching is placed within the cultural, historical, and theological contexts of baptistic communities. This research has revealed that, although preaching is generally perceived as a tool for inspirational or educational use, it has a far more complex nature in shaping various areas of church life and practice. My hope is that this work will contribute to further development of how preaching is taught and practiced in Russia's educational institutions and, subsequently, in local Baptist communities.

Conclusion

Let me draw a conclusion now. Although the purpose of this book was not meant to be a development of a new homiletical method, the concluding chapter presented some practical comments and suggestions, related to the development of this practice in Russian Baptist churches. The argument of chapter 8 was that as a powerful practice, preaching requires a community of interpreters, as well as a wider cluster of practices of reading the Bible within the community in order to nullify its destructive potential. Therefore, I have suggested that it might be possible to draw some positive lessons from the formative period of the Russian baptistic movement, when preaching was instrumental in bringing its participants to actively participate in the process of biblical interpretation. Such communal involvement in the discovery of biblical narrative and its application to the

---

29. Ibid., 398.
30. McClendon, *Ethics,* 2nd ed., 35–36.

lives of individual Christians and whole congregations resulted in a formation of clearly defined ecclesial identity, despite the resistance of various oppressive forces that were present in the surrounding culture. Thus, in light of today's crisis of identity that can be observed in local churches, such reference to the practice, still present (the phenomenon of multiple preaching) and, moreover, occupying the central part of church life, may lead to a rediscovery of the communal nature of biblical interpretation, thus restoring the lost critical edge for people's perception of the sermons, and the subsequent growth of quality preaching.

Whilst hoping that this work might be of immediate assistance for local churches, its focus, first of all, must be seen in theological educational institutions. However, when addressing the nature and place of contemporary theological education in Russia, it is impossible not to address the existing tensions in the relationship between the church and the university.

The leadership of the Baptist Union in the post-Soviet era made numerous attempts to develop preaching (and other ministries) in churches by offering educational opportunities and supporting the appearance of multiple educational institutions around Russia. However, often these attempts were downplayed by pastors in local churches. The promotion of education was seen as a threat to their position (since good preaching was always perceived a result of the work of the Holy Spirit, the need to change anything/continue learning for a pastor, implied that he was not close enough to God). As a result, people that were not needed or wanted in churches were sent to preaching schools and seminaries. Their preaching, when they returned, was neither accepted nor approved by pastors (and, hence, by congregations), causing conflicts and frustration, both in local churches and educational institutions.

However, apart from the seemingly reactionary stance taken by the local churches, the approach to teaching preaching employed by educational institutions has also contributed to the church-university divide. Neglecting the views on character formation and preparation for ministry dominant in churches, theological schools attempted to teach preaching by developing students' hermeneutical and rhetorical skills.

I have argued that to bridge the seemingly inevitable conflict between the church and the university, it is necessary to begin ministerial training with a course on Baptist identity, which would enable students to have a better understanding of the ecclesial tradition they are coming from or hoping to serve. This brings me to the second important element of theological education—the need to understand the theological task as discovery, interpretation, and potential correction of the convictions of a convictional community. Such understanding, first of all, highlights the self-involving character of theological enquiry. It also underlines the important role of the church as a community of reference, thus leading students to a greater appreciation of the existing convictions and practices of the church, and therefore enabling them to see the continuity between their studies and the ministries of local communities of faith.

Conclusion

I HAVE BELONGED TO a Baptist church since my childhood. My parents were baptized in their youth and have always been actively involved in the various ministries of a local church in the city of Voronezh and, later, in missionary work in the Voronezh, Tambov, and Lipetsk areas in Russia. It is not surprising that the church features prominently in a lot of my childhood memories. Now preaching has never ranked highly among these memories. On the contrary, sermons were something I would rather have avoided. Nonetheless, just like many other Christians, I ended up listening to (or, at least being present at) a great deal of preaching: three sermons in every service (and up to six on special occasions, such as Christmas or Easter). One of the questions I could not find an answer to was "why preaching?" What was the value of people listening to sermons, and, in particular, to so many sermons? The traditional response, that preaching was the word of God, was not satisfactory, as I could not believe God's word could have been so boring, and, often, plainly meaningless.

To a certain degree, this project is an attempt to answer that question from my childhood. The book examines the practice of proclamation in Russian Baptist communities, and the question of Baptist identity, with the aim to develop a critical analytical tool, which could be used by, first of all, educational institutions, but also the local churches, involved in the reflection and development of various church practices, and particularly, the practice of preaching. In my research, I have primarily focused on preaching as a social practice in a MacIntyrean sense. The content of preaching is mostly omitted, which is intentional, as, I believe, it deserves another dedicated study, which I hope may grow out of this research.

The first five chapters of the book are an inquiry into the question of Russian Baptist identity, with preaching playing an important role in the forming and passing on of this identity. This is, largely, a historical overview, which identifies various internal and external factors that have significantly influenced the development of baptistic communities and their worship practices. I am employing the theological method of James McClendon, who argued that the material that theology works with is convictions, expressed in a particular way of life. Thus, I focus on the history of Russian Baptists, in order to identify the convictions that are at the core of their identity.

Chapter 1 maps the historical context of the emerging Russian baptistic movement. Reforms initiated by Emperor Alexander II, the crisis that broke out in the Orthodox Church and then spread throughout the wider society, and the publishing of the Bible in the contemporary Russian language, which was made freely available—all of these factors have contributed to the appearance of the baptistic groups in the Russian Empire, which initially could be seen as a reformation movement within the Orthodox Church. Using the example of the early peasant Stundist communities, I have argued that, despite the fact that these groups were disjointed and somewhat chaotic in structure and teaching, they shared one major characteristic feature—communal preaching in the form of a simplistic literal reading of the Bible with its immediate application to the lives of the members of these communities. Suspicion and rejection that these evangelistic groups experienced from the Orthodox clergy were among the major factors that eventually caused their break-away from the established church, leading to the formation of new denominations. Thus, without rejecting the important contribution of various European evangelicals, it is possible to speak about the practice of preaching playing a prominent, formative role in the appearance and spread of the first baptistic churches in Russia.

Chapter 2 seeks to establish a theological background from which Russian baptistic communities had emerged and begun to grow. Context—a set of unique historical, sociological, political, and theological settings—inevitably influences the development of any community of faith. The vast cultural and ecclesial heritage of the Orthodox Church, which has penetrated all aspects of Russian culture, must be taken into consideration in any attempt to gain a deeper understanding of Baptist convictions and practices. In my

Conclusion

work, I have concentrated on three distinct elements of Orthodox theology and practice: theosis, *sobornost*, and the charismatic preaching.

Understanding these concepts helps to shed light on the existing reverent attitude to the church prevalent among Russian Baptists, and their unwillingness to be involved in any kind of critical analysis or evaluation of either the practices of the church or its leadership, instead emphasizing the need to have a right heart, mind, and spirit, when it comes to worship. The ideas of charismatic preaching, which dominated the Orthodox homiletical scene in the second half of the nineteenth century, bring forward a specific understanding of preaching—a sacramental act of transmitting God's words—but, more importantly, an almost mystical channel of God's grace. The subsequent chapters show that such views have significantly impacted baptistic understanding and the practice of preaching.

Chapters 3 and 4 trace the development of Russian Baptist preaching from their formative years until the collapse of the Soviet ideology, and the beginning of a new era in the history of the church. I have argued that throughout history, the baptistic understanding of preaching and its practical implications underwent substantial changes, due to the shifting political environment that the church existed within. The formative period of the baptistic movement is marked by preaching as a simplistic retelling of the biblical story with ethical application to the lives of the listeners. The absence of strict doctrinal constraints contributed to the fast growth of the movement, when the government allowed more freedom to the dissenters.

Eventually, such freedom in the use of the Scripture started to cause controversies and problems within the movement, thus highlighting the need of greater theological coherence among the diverse congregations of Baptists and Evangelical Christians. The church leaders attempted to tackle these problems by organizing training opportunities for the pastors and missionaries, and through extensive publishing activities. Magazines and newspapers enabled tens of thousands of people across the vast territory of the country to access theological essays and sermons by providing educational materials and helping achieve greater unity in the local churches. At this stage, preaching was seen as an activity, where the supernatural work of the Holy Spirit was complemented by the knowledge and preparations of the preacher. Education and personal growth were seen as important parts of the preaching ministry.

The period of persecutions, which started soon after the Bolsheviks seized power in 1917, marked another shift in how preaching (among other ministries of the church) was practiced. The impossibility of carrying out educational work and the strictly enforced ban on social and youth ministries allowed Christians to successfully rival aggressive Soviet domination only in such areas as spirituality and moral living. All of this has inevitably impacted preaching. The only available way to learn how to preach was through prayer and personal reflection, the main preparation was also through prayer, and the success of the preaching ministry was measured by the preacher's integrity and spiritual maturity. Eventually, such attitudes led to a situation where preachers were seen as special men of God, and their pulpit ministry was seen as a sign of God's calling and anointing.

Chapter 5 focuses on the post-Soviet period in the history of Russian Baptists. I briefly address topics related to the context of worship, such as the liturgy, sacred space, and participants. However, the main goal of this section is to continue developing the themes of preachers' spirituality, authority, and the listeners' perception of the act of preaching. The main argument in this chapter is that the practice of proclamation plays a much greater role in churches than that of an educational or an inspirational instrument. Culturally inherent perception of the church leadership as "holy people, unable to err," leads to the formation of a separate class of people within the presumably nonhierarchical structure of the Baptist communities. *Sluzhiteli* receive their authority through, first of all, the preaching office. Furthermore, the existing pattern of uncritical perception of the sermons, supported and encouraged by many preachers, opens the doors to various abuses of power in churches due to the absence of educated listeners and lay members, able to hold its leadership accountable. Thus, the neglect of issues of power and authority, which the preaching office attributes to its practitioners, affects the development of the contemporary churches.

Chapter 6 begins with an attempt to define the constants that constitute baptistic identity, something that preaching is primarily concerned with. I have employed the concept of the baptist vision, as developed by McClendon. The vision is understood as a particular hermeneutical principle, when the church sees itself as a part of the biblical story, whilst at the same time being examined and transformed by it. Since such approach to the baptistic identity highlights the crucial role of the Bible, the important question that has to be addressed is how this book is read by the believing community. This introduces the focus of chapter 7: the practices of reading the Bible.

Conclusion

I approach the notion of practices following MacIntyre's philosophical views. He sees social practices as something inherently positive. Participation in practices leads to the discovery of goods internal, and develops virtues. McClendon introduces an important corrective here, arguing that every practice has a potential to fall. Hence practices should be seen as powerful practices, to emphasize their constructive potential as well as hidden destructive forces. Therefore, preaching must be understood as a powerful practice, since it may result in virtues as well as in vices. From the history of Russian Baptists it can be seen how preaching changed from a communal practice, open to all, to a power attribute, available to a specially selected group of people, often alienating lay Christians from in-depth involvement with the Bible. Considering that the baptist vision, as formulated by McClendon, is a form of communal hermeneutics, preaching, in its contemporary form, can be seen as possessing powers, deforming the identity of Baptist communities.

The important question that this discussion has led to, is the question of safeguarding against potential weaknesses of proclamation, with its holding a central place in Russian Baptist worship. This strategy can be found in the practice of Bible reading, since this practice contains the necessary correctives to other vulnerable practices of the believing community, including the practice of Bible reading itself. The whole of chapter 8, therefore, becomes a case for communal hermeneutics. I have argued that in order to nullify the destructive potential of preaching, it must be utilized within a wider cluster of practices of reading the Bible, which includes the need for the whole Christian fellowship to be involved in the process of hermeneutics, developing into a community of interpreters, which involves both formal and church-based educational opportunities for its members, similar in spirit to the baptistic experiments at the beginning of the twentieth century.

Since Baptists perceive the Bible to be the Holy Scripture, rather than a mere ancient text, they employ reading strategies which are different from the hermeneutical tools used in academic study. The church, first of all, seeks literal and spiritual senses in the biblical text, through its typological reading. Their safeguarding strategy against potential misinterpretations is reading the Scripture in a community of fellow Christians, under the guidance of the Holy Spirit. Thus, the conclusions of this chapter are, first of all, a theological justification for an argument that reading the Bible in the community, understood and practiced within a wider cluster of practices, and preaching as one of them, serves as a sufficient safeguarding strategy against the destructive potential of various powerful practices, including the practice of proclamation.

The final chapter aims to address the question of what kind of preaching is required, in light of the previous discussion of the powerful practices, and the call for the church to rediscover the communal aspect in biblical interpretation. I have argued that an important lesson might be drawn from the existing phenomenon of multiple acts of preaching in one service. However, instead of focusing on its present form, I believe it is necessary to look into the formative years of the movement, which could be seen as a successful experiment in communal hermeneutics, with proclamation being the formative force behind the emergence of a particular ecclesial identity, despite the resistance of the dominant religious culture and political establishment.

It is worth restating that this book was not meant to offer a new homiletical method. If anything, this is a call to reevaluate the existing emphasis on preaching as the practice, responsible for the transition of the biblical narrative into the lives of the listeners. The rediscovery of the communal aspect of biblical interpretation necessitates significant shifts in the churches' understanding of various theological convictions, and particularly questions of leadership and authority. Therefore, practical implications of this study must first of all be seen in theological educational institutions, which are involved in the preparation of preachers and pastors, but also aim to be places of the furthering of theological thought.

An overview of the curriculums of two major theological schools highlights that students are being taught the discipline of homiletics with the main emphasis on biblical exegesis and rhetoric, based primarily on materials, developed in Anglo-American context, therefore lacking the understanding of the ecclesial tradition they are coming from or aspiring to minister to, which inevitably contributes to the still unbridged chasm between the church and the university. To address this issue the schools need to introduce deeper studies of the Baptist identity, as well as perform a shift in their approach to the theological task, which needs to be seen as a discovery, an interpretation, and the potential correction of the convictions of the church. I believe these amendments would result in an enhanced understanding, and therefore a greater appreciation by the academic institutions of the existing convictions and practices of local churches, and, hence, make mutual enrichment and development possible.

Bibliography

Adam, A. K. M. *Faithful Interpretation: Reading the Bible in a Postmodern Word*. Minneapolis: Fortress, 2006.
Aghiorgoussis, Maximos. "The Theology and Experience of Salvation." *Greek Orthodox Theological Review* 22 (1977) 405–15.
Amvrosii, Archbishop (Alexei Klucharev). *Zhivoie slovo (Living Word)*. Kharkov, Ukraine: Izdaniie Soveta Kharkovskogo Eparhialnogo Zhenskogo Uchilischa, 1903.
Andronoviene, Lina, and Parush R. Parushev. "Church, State, and Culture: On the Complexities of Post-Soviet Evangelical Social Involvement." *Theological Reflections* 3 (2004) 194–212.
Antonenko, Victoria. "Principles for Interpreting Jesus' Parables and the Way they are Understood by Evangelical Christians in Russia." *Theological Reflections* 4 (2004) 76–95.
Applebaum, Anne. *Gulag: A History of the Soviet Camps*. Garden City, NY: Doubleday, 2003.
Bakker, Hank. "Convictional Theology as Mapping Moral Space." *Baptistic Theologies* 6.1 (2014) 81–97.
Bartos, Emil. *Deification in Eastern Orthodox Theology: An Evaluation and Critique of the Theology of Dumitru Staniloae*. Milton Keynes, UK: Paternoster, 1999.
Berger, Peter L. *The Sacred Canopy*. Garden City, NY: Doubleday, 1967.
———. *The Social Construction of Reality*. Garden City, NY: Doubleday, 1966.
Bilaniuk, Petro, "The Mystery of Theosis or Divinization." In *The Heritage of the Early Church: Essay in Honor of the Very Reverend Georges Vasilievich Florovsky*, edited by David Neiman and Margaret Schatkin. Rome: Pont. Institutum Stadiorum Orientalium, 1973.
Birch, Ian. "Baptists and Biblical Interpretation: Reading the Bible with Christ." In *The Plainly Revealed Word of God? Baptist Hermeneutics in Theory and Practice*, edited by Helen Dare and Simon Woodman. Macon, GA: Mercer University Press, 2011.
Black, Cyril E., ed. *The Transformation of Russian Society: Aspects of Social Change since 1861*. Cambridge: Harvard University Press, 1960.
Bokova, Olga A. "Bibleiskaia ekzegetika i germenevtika sovremennikh evangelskikh khristian – baptistov: traditsii i novatsii" ("Biblical exegetics and hermeneutics of contemporary Evangelical Christians–Baptists: traditions and new trends"). *Vestnik Leningradskogo Gosudarstvennogo Universiteta im. A. S. Pushkina* 2.2 (2013) 125–32.
Borovoy, Vitaly. "What is Salvation? An Orthodox Statement." *International Review of Mission* 61 (1972) 38–45.

Bibliography

Brackney, William H. *The Baptists.* New York: Greenwood, 1988.

Brandenburg, Hans. *The Meek and the Mighty: The Emergence of the Evangelical Movement in Russia.* New York: Oxford University Press, 1977.

Brown, David M. *Transformational Preaching: Theory and Practice.* College Station, TX: Virtualbookworm.com, 2003.

Buss, Andreas E. *The Russian-Orthodox Tradition and Modernity.* Leiden, the Netherlands: Brill, 2003.

Callahan, James P. *Primitivist Piety: The Ecclesiology of the Early Plymouth Brethren.* Lanham, MD: Scarecrow, 1996.

Campbell, Charles L. *Preaching Jesus: The New Directions for Homiletics in Hans Frei's Postliberal Theology.* Eugene, OR: Wipf & Stock, 1997.

———. *The Word Before the Powers: An Ethics of Preaching.* Louisville: Westminster John Knox, 1999.

Cheprasov, Timofey. "Back to the Future: The Discovery of the Future of Russian Baptist Social Involvement through the Narratives of the Past." *Baptistic Theologies* 3.2 (2011) 88–99.

———. "Church Discipline." In *A Dictionary of European Baptist Life and Thought*, edited by John H. Y. Briggs. Milton Keynes, UK: Paternoster, 2009.

———. "Political and Religious Factors in the Emergence of the Baptist Movement in the Russian Empire." *Baptistic Theologies* 2.2 (2010) 46–58.

Cherenkov, Mykhailo. "Nash baptism: istoriia i sovremennost" ("Our Baptism: History and Modern Era"), 12 December 2009, http://cherenkoff.blogspot.com/2009/11/blog-post.html.

———. "Post-Soviet Protestants between the Church and the University." *Theological Reflections,* Special edition: Bible, Theology, Church (2013) 23–30.

Coleman, Heather J. "The Most Dangerous Sect: Baptists in Tsarist and Soviet Russia, 1905–1929." PhD diss., University of Illinois at Urbana-Champaign, 1998.

———. *Russian Baptists and Spiritual Revolution, 1905–1929.* Indianapolis: Indiana University Press, 2005.

Conquest, Robert. *The Great Terror: A Reassessment.* Oxford: Oxford University Press, 1990.

Corrado, Sheryl. *Filosofiia sluzheniia polkovnika Pashkova (The Philosophy of Ministry of Colonel Pashkov).* St. Petersburg: Biblia Dlya Vsekh, 2005.

———. "The Gospel in Society: Pashkovite Social Outreach in Late Imperial Russia." In *Eastern European Baptist History: New Perspectives*, edited by Sheryl Corrado and Toivo Pilli, 52–70. Prague: IBTS, 2007.

Craddock, Fred B. *Preaching.* Nashville: Abingdon, 1985.

Dawn, Marva. "The Biblical Concept of the 'Principalities and Powers': John Yoder Points to Jacques Ellul." In *The Wisdom of the Cross: Essays in Honor of John Howard Yoder.* edited by Stanley Hauerwas et al., 168–88. Grand Rapids: Eerdmans, 1999.

———. *Powers, Weakness, and the Tabernacle of God.* Grand Rapids: Eerdmans, 2001.

Dementiev, Andrei. *Evangelskoie dvizheniie v Primorie: 1898–1990 (Evangelical Movement in the Far-East of Russia:1898–1990),* Vladivostok, Russia: Russkii Ostrov, 2011.

Dick, Viktor. *Svet evangeliia v Kazakhstane: istoriia vosvessheniia evangeliia i rasprostraneniia obshin baptistov i menonnitov v Kazakhstane. Pervaia polovina XX veka (The Light of the Gospel in Kazakhstan: The History of the Proclamation of the Gospel and the Spreading of the Baptist and Mennonite Communities in Kazakhstan. First Half of the XX Century),* Samenkorn, Germany: Steinhagen, 2003.

BIBLIOGRAPHY

Doronitsin, Alexii. *Materiali dlia istorii vozniknovenia i rasprostroneniia stundi na yuge Rossii (Materia's for the History of the Appearance and Spread of the Stundist Movement in the South of Russia),* Kazan, Russia: Kievskaia Starina, 1884.

Durasoff, Steve. *The Russian Protestants: Evangelicals in the Soviet Union, 1944–1964.* Madison, NJ: Fairleigh Dickinson University Press, 1969.

Dyck, Johanness. "Molding the Brotherhood: Johann Wieler (1839–1889): And the Communities of the Early Evangelicals in Russia." MTh diss., IBTS, 2007.

Elliot, Mark. "Bogoslovskoie obrazovaniie v postkommunisticheskii period: polozhitelniie i otritsatelniie storony zapadnoi pomoschi" ("Theological Education in Post-communistic Period: Positive and Negative Sides of Western Help"). *Put Bogopoznaniia* 1 (1996) 17–25.

Ellis, Geoff, and Wesley Jones. *The Other Revolution. Russian Evangelical Awakening.* Abilene, TX: Abilene Christian University Press, 1996.

Ermolov, I. G. "Evangelskie khristiane–baptisti v period okupatsii RSFSR 1941–1944" ("Evangelical Christians–Baptists During the Period of Occupation of Russian Federation in 1941–1944"). In *105 let legalizatsii russkogo baptisma (105 Years of Legalization of Russian Baptism),* edited by Nadezhda A. Beliakova and Alexey V. Sinichkin, 173–79. Moscow: RUECB, 2011.

Esaulov, Ivan A. "Sobornost v filosofii A. S. Khomyakova i sovremennaia Rossiia" ("Sobornost in Philosophy of A. S. Khomyakov and Modern Russia"). In *A.S. Khomyakov—mislitel, poet, publitsist,* edited by Boris Tarasov, 11–17. Moscow: Iaziki Slovianskoi Kulturi 2007.

Fadyukhin, Sergei P. "Sovety propovednikam" ("Recommendations to Preachers"). *Bratskii Vestnik* 5 (1965) 33–44.

Fedotov, Georgy. *The Russian Religious Mind: Kievan Christianity. The Tenth to the Thirteenth Centuries.* Vol. 3. Belmont, MA: Nordland, 1975.

Feoktistov, Evgenii M. *Vospominaniia. Zakulisami politiki i literatury 1848—1896 (Memoirs: Behind the Curtains of Politics and Literature 1848-1896),* Leningrad: Priboi, 1929.

Fetzer, Johann G. "Baptists in Russia and what They Need." *Baptist Missionary Magazine* 83 (April 1903) 126–28.

Fish, Stanley. *Doing what Comes Naturally: Change, Rhetoric, and the Practice of Theory in Literary and Legal Studies.* Durham, NC: Duke University Press, 1989.

Florenskii, Pavel. "Poniatiie tserkvi v sviaschennom pisanii" ("The Concept of the Church in the Holy Scripture") *Bogoslovskiie Trudy* 12 (1974) 78–183.

Florovsky, Georges V. "Dukhovnie razmishleniia" ("Spiritual reflections"). http://www.pravbeseda.ru/library/index.php?page=book&id=783.

———. *Puti russkogo bogoslovia (Ways of Russian Theology).* Moscow: Institute of Russian Civilization, 2009.

Fowl, Stephen E. and L. Gregory Jones. *Reading in Communion: Scripture and Ethics in Christian Life.* Grand Rapids: Eerdmans, 1991.

———. "Scripture, Exegesis, and Discernment in Christian Ethics." In *Virtues and Practices in the Christian Tradition: Christian Ethics After MacIntyre,* edited by Nancy C. Murphy et al., 111–31. Valley Forge, PA: Trinity Press International, 1997.

Freeze, Gregory L. "Reform and Counter Reform 1855–1890." In *Russia, A History,* 2nd ed., edited by Gregory L. Freeze, 199–233. Oxford: Oxford University Press, 2002.

Frei, Hans W. *The Eclipse of Biblical Narrative: A Study in Eighteenth and Nineteenth Century Hermeneutics.* New Haven, CT: Yale University Press, 1974.

Bibliography

———. *Types of Christian Theology*. Edited by George Hunsinger and William C. Placher. New Haven, CT: Yale University Press, 1992.

George, Archimandrite. *Theosis: The True Purpose of Human Life*. Mount Athos, Greece: Holy Monastery of St. Gregorios, 2006.

Grams, Rolling G., and Parush R. Parushev, eds. *Towards an Understanding of European Baptist Identity: Listening to the Churches in Armenia, Bulgaria, Central Asia, Moldova, North Caucasus, Omsk and Poland*. Prague: IBTS, 2006.

Harrink, Douglas. *Paul among the Postliberals: Pauline Theology Beyond Christendom and Modernity*. Grand Rapids: Brazos, 2003.

Harris, Mark J. "Toward an Understanding of Russian Baptist Preaching." http://cvi2.org/pages/harris/harris_russian_baptist_preaching1996.pdf.

Harvey, Barry, "'This as That': Friendly Amendments to James McClendon's 'Baptist' Vision." *Baptistic Theologies* 6.1 (2014) 36–52.

Hatchett, Randy. "The Hermeneutics of Conversion." In *Ties That Bind: Life Together in the Baptist Vision*, edited by Gary Furr and Curtis W. Freeman. Macon, GA: Smyth and Helwys, 1994.

Hauerwas, Stanley. "Christianity: It's an Adventure." In *The Hauerwas Reader*, edited by John Berkman and Michael Cartwright. Durham, NC: Duke University Press, 2001.

———. *A Community of Character: Toward a Constructive Christian Social Ethic*. Notre Dame, IN: University of Notre Dame Press, 1981.

Hebly, Johannes A. *Protestants in Russia,*.Belfast: Christian Journals Limited, 1976.

Heier, Edmund. *Religious Schism in the Russian Aristocracy 1860–1900: Radstockism and Pashkovism*. Hague: Nimhoff, 1970.

Humphreys, Fisher. *The Way We Were: How Southern Baptist Theology has Changed and What it Means to Us All*. Macon, GA: Smyth and Helwys, 2002.

Istoriia evangelskikh khristian-baptistov v SSSR (The History of the Evangelical Christians-Baptists in the USSR). Moscow: VSEKHB, 1989.

Iswolsky, Helene. *Christ in Russia: The History, Tradition, and Life of the Russian Church*. Milwaukee: The Bruce, 1960.

Ivanov, Vasilii V. "Pozlozheniie baptistov" ("The situation Baptists are in"). *Baptist* 9 (1911) 69–71.

Jensen, Richard A. *Envisioning the Word: The Use of Visual Images in Preaching*. Minneapolis: Augsburg, 2005.

Jones, Keith G. "Baptists and Anabaptists Revisited." In *Exploring Baptist Origins*, edited by Anthony R. Cross and Nicholas J. Wood. Oxford: Regent's Park, 2010.

———. "Towards a Model of Mission for Gathering, Intentional, Convictional Koinonia." *Journal of European Baptist Studies* 4.2 (2004) 5–13.

Kallenberg, Brad J. "The Master Argument of MacIntyre's After Virtue." In *Virtues and Practices in the Christian Tradition: Christian Ethics After MacIntyre*, edited by Nancy C. Murphy et al., 7–29. Valley Forge, PA: Trinity Press International, 1997.

Karetnikova, Marina S. "U istokov sovremennogo religioznogo obrazovaniia v Rossii" ("At the Roots of Contemporary Religious Education in Russia"). In *Traditsiia podgotovki sluzhitelei v bratstve evangelskikh khristian-baptistov. Istoriia i perspectivi: sbornik statei (Tradition of Preparation of Ministers in the Brotherhood of Evangelical Christians–Baptists. History and Prospects: Collection of Articles)*. Moscow: RUECB, 2013.

Karev, Aexander V. "Russkoie evangelsko-baptistskoie dvizheniie" ("Russian Evangelical-Baptist Movement"). In *Al'manakh po istorii russkogo baptisma: russkoie*

Bibliography

bogoiskatelstvo (Almanac on the History of Russian Baptists: Russian Search for God), vol. 1, edited by Marina S. Karetnikova, 85–186. St. Petersburg: Bibliya Dlia Vsekh, 1999.

———. "V pomoshch propovednikam" ("To Assist Preachers"). *Bratskii Vestnik* 2 (1954) 65–79.

Karev, Alexander, et al. *Ekzegetika* (Exegesis). Moscow: VSEKHB, 1966.

Kargel, Ivan. "V kakom t. otnoshenii k dukhu sviatomu" ("What is Your Relationship to the Holy Spirit") In *Sobranie sochinenii* (*The Collection of Works*), 114–79. St. Petersburg: Biblia Dlya Vsekh, 1997.

Katunskii, Alexander. *Staroobriadchestvo* (*Old Believers*). Moscow: IPL, 1972.

Khlevnyuk, Oleg V. *Politburo: Mekhanizmi politicheskoi vlasti v 30-e godi* (*Politburo Mechanisms of Political Power in 1930s*). Moscow: ROSSPEN, 1996.

Khomyakov, Alexey S. "Opit Katechezicheskogo izlozheniia ucheniia o tserkvi." In *Polnoie sobraniie sochinenii*, ("An Example of Catechetical Presentation of the Teaching of the Church", in *Full Collection of Writings*), vol. 2. 3rd ed. Moscow: ROSSPEN, 1886.

———. *Polnoie sobranie sochinenii* (*Full Collection of Writings*), vol. 2. Prague: Universitetskaya Tipografiia, 1867.

Khorunjii, Sergei. *Posle pereriva: Puti russikoi filosofii* (*After the Break: The Ways of Russian Philosophy*). St. Petersburg: Alteja, 1994.

Kieckhefer, Richard. *Theology in Stone: Church Architecture from Byzantium to Berkeley*. New York: Oxford University Press, 2004.

Kireyevskii, Ivan V. *Polnoie sobranie sochinenii* (*Full Collection of Writings*), vol. 2. Moscow: Tipografiia Imperskogo Moskovskogo Universiteta, 1911.

Klippenste, Lawrence. "Russian Evangelicalism Revisited: Ivan Kargel and the Founding of the Russian Baptist Union." *Baptist History and Heritage* 27.2 (1992) 42–48.

Komarov, Anton. "Evangelskiie christiane-baptisti v sisteme gosudarstvenno-religioznikh otnoshenii v SSSR: 1944–63 gg" ("Evangelical Christians-Baptists in the system of State-Religious Relationships in USSR: 1944–63"). Evrasiia: Dukhovniie Traditsii Narodov (Eurasia: Spiritual Traditions of the Nations), 2012.

Kornilov, N. A. "Kakogo roda bogosloviiа nam nuzhno?" ("What Kind of Theology do We Need?"). *Put Bogopoznaniia* 6 (2000) 5–17.

———. "K voprosu ob avtoritete v khristianskoi zhizni" ("To the Question of Authority in Christian Life"). *Put Bogopoznaniia* 2 (1997) 14–42.

Kosinko, Alexander. "Stanovleniie bogoslovskogo obrazovaniia kak osushchestvleniie dukhovnikh chaianii evangelskogo bratstva" ("Formation of Theological Education as Fulfillment of Dreams of Evangelical Brotherhood"). *Put Bogopoznaniia* 1 (1996) 6–16.

Krizhanovskii, Rostislav. *Kto takiie baptisty?* (*Who are Baptists?*). Irpen, Ukraine: Dukhovnoie Vozrozhdeniie, 2012.

Kushnev, Ivan. *Nemetskiie very* (*German Faiths*). Orel, Russia: Tipographia A. A. Logunova, 1916.

Kutepov, Nikolaii. *Kratkaia istoriia i verоucheniie russkikh ratsionalisticheskikh i misticheskikh eresei* (*Short History and Beliefs of Russian Rationalistic and Mystical Sects*). Moscow: Tipografiia E. Lissnera i Y. Romana, 1891.

Kuznetsov, G. A. "Nashi evangelskie zhurnaly" ("Our Gospel Journals"). *Bratskii Vestnik* 5 (1965) 65–70.

Bibliography

Kuznetsova, Miriam R. "Early Russian Evangelicals (1874–1929): Historical Background and Hermeneutical Tendencies Based on I. V. Kargel's Written Heritage." PhD Diss., University of Pretoria, 2009.

Latimer, Robert Sloan. *Dr. Braedek and His Apostolic Work in Russia*. London: Morgan and Scott, 1908.

Leonard, Bill J. "Eschatology." In *A Baptist's Theology*, edited by R. Wayne Stacy, 191–208. Macon, GA: Smyth and Helwys, 1999.

Leskov, Nicolay. *Schism in High Society: Lord Radstock and His Followers*, Nottingham, UK: Bramcote, 1995.

Lieven, Sofia. *Dukhovnoie probuzdeniie v Rossii (Spiritual Awakening in Russia)*. Korntal, Germany: Svet na Vostoke, 1967.

Lingenfelter, Sherwood G., and Marvin K. Mayers. *Ministering Cross Culturally: An Incarnational Model for Personal Relationships*. Grand Rapids: Baker, 2003.

Lloyd-Jones, D. Martyn. *Preaching and Preachers*. London: Hodder and Stoughton, 1971.

MacIntyre, Alasdair. *After Virtue*, 2nd ed. Notre Dame, IN: University of Notre Dame Press, 1984.

———. "Epistemological Crises, Dramatic Narrative, and the Philosophy of Science." In *Why Narrative: Readings in Narrative Theology*, edited by Stanley Hauerwas and L. Gregory Jones. Grand Rapids: Eerdmans, 1989.

Margaritov, Sergei. *Istoriia russkikh misticheskikh i ratsionalisticheskikh sect (The History of Russian Mystical and Rationalistic Sects)*. Simpheropol: Tavricheskaia Gubernskaia Tipografiia, 1910.

Masin, E. "Presviter dolzhen bit osviashchen Gospodom" ("Presbyter Must be Sanctified by God"). *Bratskii Vestnik* 2 (1959) 55–61.

Mazaev, Dei. "O dukhovnikh seminariakh" ("About Spiritual Seminaries"). *Gost* 4 (1912) 18–19.

McClendon, James Wm., Jr. "The Baptist Vision." *Baptistic Theologies* 6.1 (2014) 23–35.

———. *Biography as Theology: How Life Stories can Remake Today's Theology*. Nashville: Abingdon, 1974.

———. *Doctrine: Systematic Theology, Volume II*. Nashville: Abingdon, 1994.

———. *Ethics: Systematic Theology, Volume I*. 1986. Reprint, Waco, TX: Baylor University Press, 2012.

———. *Ethics: Systematic Theology, Volume I*, 2nd ed. Nashville: Abingdon, 2002.

———. "A New Way to Read the Bible." In *The Collected Works of James Wm. McClendon, Jr.*, vol. 2, edited by Ryan Andrew Newson and Andrew C. Wright. Waco, TX: Baylor University Press, 2014.

———. "The Practice of Community Formation." In *Virtues and Practices in the Christian Tradition: Christian Ethics After MacIntyre*, edited by Nancy C. Murphy et al., 85–110. Valley Forge, PA: Trinity Press International, 1997.

———. *Witness: Systematic Theology, Volume III*. Nashville: Abingdon, 2000.

McClendon, James Wm., Jr., and James M. Smith. *Convictions: Defusing Religious Relativism*. Reprint. Eugene: Wipf & Stock, 2002.

McKnight, Edgar. *The Bible and the Reader: An Introduction to Literary Criticism*. Philadelphia: Fortress, 1985.

———. *Postmodern Use of the Bible: The Emergence of Reader-oriented Criticism*. Nashville: Abingdon, 1988.

Michels, Georg Bernard. *At War with the Church: Religious Dissent in Seventeenth-Century Russia*. Stanford, CA: Stanford University Press, 1999.

Bibliography

Mikhovich, Leonid. "Compatibility of Theology and Practice of Traditional Public Worship in Baptist Churches in Belarus." Forthcoming doctoral dissertation for the award of PhD degree, Vrije Universiteit, Amsterdam.

Mitrokhin, Lev N. *Baptism: istoriia i sovremennost (Filosofsko-sotsiologicheskiie ocherki) (Baptist Movement: History and Contemporary Situation [Philosophical-Sociological Articles])*. St. Petersburg: Rossiiskaia Khristianskaia Gumanitarnaia Akademiia, 1997.

Mitskevich, Artur I. *Istoriia evangelskikh khristian-baptistov (History of Evangelical Christians-Baptists)*. Moscow: RUECB, 2007.

———. "Vseobshcheie sviashchenstvo i sluzhiteli tserkvi" ("Priesthood of all Believers and Church Ministers"). *Bratskii Vestnik* 3 (1965) 29–36.

M. N. "Velika nagrada vasha na nebesakh" ("Your Reward in Heaven is Great"). *Bratskii Vestnik* 5 (1985) 12–15.

Moltmann, Jürgen. *The Church in the Power of the Spirit*. New York: Harper and Row, 1975.

Motorin, Ivan. "Bibliia—slovo Bozhiie" ("Bible–the Word of God"). *Bratskii Vestnik* 4 (1946) 4–6.

———. "Kak izuchat bibliyu" ("How to Study the Bible"). *Bratskii Vestnik* 5 (1947) 56–60.

———. "Nekotoriie ukazaniia o tom, kak gotovitsia k propovedi" ("Some Instructions on how to Prepare for Preaching"). *Bratskii Vestnik* 2 (1948) 53–57.

———. "Sluzheniie propovednika" ("Preacher's Ministry"). *Bratskii Vestnik* 1 (1954) 30–44.

Mullins, Edgar Y. *Baptist Beliefs*. Valley Forge, PA: Judson, 1912.

Murphy, Nancy C. "Using MacIntyre's Method in Christian Ethics." In *Virtues and Practices in the Christian Tradition: Christian Ethics After MacIntyre*, edited by Nancy C. Murphy et al., 30–44. Harrisburg, PA: Trinity Press International, 1997.

Nagirniak, Alexander. "Bibleiskiie kursy baptistov v Moskve v 1927–1929 godakh" ("Bible Courses in Moscow in 1927–1929"). In *Traditsiia podgotovki sluzhitelei v bratstve evangelskikh khristian-baptistov: Istoriia i perspectivi: sbornik statei (Tradition of Preparation of Ministers in the Brotherhood of Evangelical Christians–Baptists: History and Prospects: Collection of Articles)*. Moscow: RUECB, 2013.

Nastol'naia kniga sviashchennika (Priest's Handbook), vol. 5. Moscow: Izdatelstvo Moskovskoi Patriarkhii, 1986.

Nichols, Gregory L. *The Development of Russian Evangelical Spirituality: A Study of Ivan V Kargel (1849-1937)*. Eugene, OR: Pickwick, 2011.

N. N. "I. S. Prokhanov kak propovednik" ("I. S. Prokhanov as a Preacher") *Bratskii Vestnik* 1 (1947) 68–70.

———. "Rabota nad propovediami" ("Work on Sermons"). *Bratskii Vestnik* 5 (1969) 52–53.

"O Sluzhenii zhenshchin v tserkvi" ("Regarding Women's Ministry in the Church"). *Bratskii Vestnik* 3 (1945) 47–49.

Ovsianiko-Kulikovskii, D. N "Kaiushchiesia dvoriane' i raznochintsy 60-kh godov" ("'The Repenting Nobles' and Razhochintsy of the 60s"). In *Istoriia russkoi intelligentsii. Sobranie Sochinenii (The history of Russian Intelligentsia. The Collection of Works)*, vol. 8. St. Petersburg: Izdaniie V. M. Sablina, 1911.

Paert, Irina. *Old Believers, Religious Dissent and Gender in Russia, 1760–1850*, Manchester, UK: Manchester University Press, 2003.

Bibliography

Panich, Olena, "Children and Childhood among Evangelical Christians-Baptists During the Late Soviet Period (1960s–1980s)." *Theological Reflections* 13 (2012) 155–79.

Parushev, Parush R. "Baptist and Society." Paper presented at the Post-graduate Seminar at IBTS as part pf the series on Baptistic identity and theology, IBTS, Prague, 24.10.2007.

———. "Baptistic Convictional Hermeneutics." In *The Plainly Revealed Word of God? Baptist Hermeneutics in Theory and Practice*, edited by Helen Dare and Simon Woodman, 172–90. Macon, GA: Mercer University Press, 2011.

———. *Christianity in Europe: The Way We are Now*. Crowther Centre Monographs Series 9. Oxford: Church Missionary Society, 2009.

———. "Romantické vlivy na počátku ruského slavjanofilského hnutí" ("Romantic Influences at the Beginnings of the Slavophile Movement in Russia"). In *Křesťanství a Romantismus* (Christianity and Romantism), vol. 15, *Quaestiones quodlibetales* series, edited by Ivana Noble and Jiří Hanuš, 64–83. Prague: Centrum pro Studium Demokrace a Kultury, 2011.

———. "Walking in the Dawn of the Light: On Salvation Ethics of the Ecclesial Communities in Orthodox Tradition from a Radical Reformation Perspective." PhD diss., Fuller Theological Seminary, 2007.

Pavlov, Vasilii G. "Pravda o baptistakh" ("The Truth about Baptists"). In *Al'manakh po istorii russkogo baptisma: russkoie bogoiskatelstvo (Almanac on the History of Russian Baptists: Russian Search for God)*, vol. 1, edited by Marina S. Karetnikova, 220–72. St. Petersburg: Biblia Dlya Vsekh, 1999.

Pavlyuk, Petr. "Destructivnoie naslediie sovetskogo proshlogo" ("Destructive Heritage of the Soviet Past"). In *105 let legalizatsii russkogo baptisma (105 Years of Legalization of Russian Baptism)*, edited by Nadezhda A. Beliakova and Alexey V. Sinichkin, 40–44. Moscow: RUECB, 2011.

Pelikan, Jaroslav. "Orthodox Theology in the West: The Reformation." In *The Legacy of St. Vladimir*, edited by John Breck et al., 159–66. Crestwood, NY: St. Vladimir's Seminary Press, 1990.

Pereligin, Anatolii. "Orlovskaia eparkhiia v 1943–1945" ("Orlov Eparchy in 1943–1945"). In *Istorii russkoi provintsii: sbornik statei (Narratives of Russian Province: Collection of Articles)*, edited by Nikolai Makarov, 342–59. St. Petersburg: Bibliopolis, 2006.

Podberezskii, Igor V. "O kalvinizme, kharismatii, voiennoi sluzhbe i mnogom mnogom drugom. S predsedateliem RSEKHB Y. K. Sipko beseduiet I. V. Podberezskii" ("About Calvinism, Charismatics, Military Service and Many Other Things: I. V. Podberezskii's Conversation with Y. K. Sipko, the President of RUECB"). *Khristianskoie slovo* 2 (2003) 34–40.

Polonskii, Yuri P. *Moi studencheskie vospominaniia (My Student Memories)*. Moscow: Prose, 1988.

Polunov, Alexander I. "Church, Regime, and Society in Russia (1880-1895)." *Russian Studies in History* 39.4 (2001) 33–53.

Popov, Alexander V. "The Evangelical Christians-Baptists in the Soviet Union as Hermeneutical Community: Examining the Identity of the All-Union Council of the ECB (AUCECB) Through the Way the Bible Was Used in its Publications." PhD Diss., IBTS, 2010.

———. "Traditsii izdatelstva VSEKHB v zhurnale 'Bratskii Vestnik'" ("The Traditions of Publication of AUCECB in *Bratskii Vestnik*"), 01 October 2007. http://web.archive.

Bibliography

org/web/20111228041553/http://rosbaptist.ru/index.php?Itemid=221&id=132&option=com_content&task=view.

Popov, Vlalimir A. "Khristianskiie komunni I. S. Prokhanova i gorod solntsa" ("Christian Communes of I. S. Prokhanov and the City of Sun"). In *105 let legalizatsii russkogo baptisma (105 Years of Legalization of Russian Baptism)*, edited by Nadezhda A. Beliakova and Alexey V. Sinichkin, 135-38. Moscow: RUECB, 2011.

———. "Otechestvenniaia shkola propovedi v tserkvakh evangelskikh khristian baptistov" ("National School of Preaching in the Churches of Evangelical Christian-Baptists"). In *Traditsiia podgotovki sluzhitelei v bratstve evangelskikh khristian-baptistov. Istoriia i perspectivi: sbornik statei (Tradition of Preparation of Ministers in the Brotherhood of Evangelical Christians-Baptists. History and Prospects: Collection of Articles)*, Moscow: RUECB, 2013.

———. "Pervii evangelskii zhurnal v rossii" ("First Evangelical Journal in Russia"). *Put Bogopoznaniia* 3 (1993) 23-29.

———. *Stopi blagovestnika: zhizn i trudi V. G. Pavlova (The Feet of the One Who Brings Good News: Life and Work of V. G. Pavlov)*. Moscow: Blagovestnik, 1996.

Potapova, Natalia. "Vosproizvodstvo kadrov sluzhitelei dalnevostochnikh baptistskikh tserkvei v usloviiakh sistemnogo crizisa 1917-1922" ("Preparation of Ministers in Baptist Churches in the Far East in the Time of Crisis of 1917-1922"). In *Traditsiia podgotovki sluzhitelei v bratstve evangelskikh khristian-baptistov. Istoriia i perspectivi: sbornik statei (Tradition of Preparation of Ministers in the Brotherhood of Evangelical Christians-Baptists. History and Prospects: Collection of Articles)*, 74-92. Moscow: RUECB, 2013.

Prokhanov, Ivan S. "Kachestva propovednika" ("Qualities of a Preacher"). *Bratskii Vestnik* 4 (1946) 18-21.

———. *Kratkoie ucheniie o propovedy: opit evangelskoy gomiletiki (Short Teaching on Preaching: Experience of Evangelical Homiletics)*. Korntal, Germany: Svet na vostoke, 1969.

———. "Poroki propovednikov" ("Vices of preachers"). *Bratskii Vestnik* 5 (1946) 47-50.

———. *V kotle Rossii 1869-1933: avtobiografiia Ivana Stepanovicha Prokhanova s izlozheniiem glavnikh faktov dvizheniia evangelskikh khristian v Rossii (In the Cauldron of Russia 1869-1933: An Autobiography of Ivan Stepanovich Prokhanov with the Narration of Main Facts Regarding the Movement of Evangelical Christians in Russia)*. Druckhaus, Germany: Gummersbach, 1992.

Prokhorov, Konstantin. *Bozie and kesarevo*. Omsk: Nauka, 2005.

———. "Russian Baptists and Orthodoxy, 1960-1990: A Comparative Study of Theology, Liturgy and Traditions." PhD Diss., IBTS, 2011.

Prokhvatilova, Olga A. *Pravoslavnaia propoved i molitva kak fenomen sovremennoi zvuchaschei rechi (Orthodox Preaching and Prayer as a Phenomenon of Contemporary Speech)*. Volgograd, Russia: Volgogradskii Gosudarstvennii Universitet, 1999.

Puzynin, Andrey. "The Tradition of the Gospel Christians: A Reconstruction of the Practice of Biblical Interpretation." *Theological Reflections* 13 (2012) 32-52.

———. *The Tradition of the Gospel Christians: A Study of Their Identity and Theology During the Russian, Soviet, and Post-Soviet Periods*. Eugene, OR: Pickwick, 2010.

Quicke, Michael J. *360 Degree Preaching*, Grand Rapids: Baker Academic, 2003.

Randall, Ian M. "Eastern European Baptists and the Evangelical Alliance, 1846-1896." In *Eastern European Baptist History: New Perspectives*, edited by Sheryl Corrado and Toivo Pilli, 14-33. Prague: IBTS, 2007.

Bibliography

Reshetnikov, Yuri, and Sergei Sannikov. *Obzor istorii evangelskogo – baptistskogo bratstva na Ukraine (The Overview of the History of the Evangelical–Baptist Brotherhood in the Ukraine)*. Odessa, Ukraine: Bogomislie, 2000.

Riasanovsky, Nicholas V. *Russian Identities: A Historical Survey*. Oxford: Oxford University Press, 2005.

Riasanovsky, Nicholas V., and Mark D. Steinberg. *A History of Russia*, 7th ed. Oxford: Oxford University Press, 2005.

Robinson, H. Wheeler. *The Life and Faith of Baptists*. London: Kingsgate, 1966.

Rozhdestvenskii, Arsenii. *Yuzhno-russkii stundism (Southern Russian Stundism)*. St. Petersburg: Tipographiia Departamenta Udelov, 1889.

Savinskii, Sergei. *Istoriia evangelskikh khristian – baptistov ukraini, Rossii, Belorussii. 1867–1917 (The History of the Evangelical Christians–Baptists of the Ukraine, Russia, Belarus. 1867–1917)*, vol. 1. St. Petersburg: Bibliia Dlya Vsech, 1999.

———. *Istoriia russko-ukrainskogo baptisma: uchebnoie posobiie (The History of Russian-Ukrainian Baptism: Study Manual)*. Odessa: Bogomislie, 1995.

Sawatsky, Walter. *Evangelicheskoie dvizheniie v SSSR posle vtoroi mirovoi voini (Evangelical Movement in USSR after World War II)*. Moscow: Garant, 1995.

———. *Soviet Evangelicals Since World War II*, Kitchener, ON: Herald, 1981.

Schavelin, V. S. "Chto dolzhen znat propovednik" ("What a Preacher Must Know"). *Bratskii Vestnik* 3–4 (1955) 69–72.

Schleiermacher, Friedrich. *The Christian Faith*. Edinburgh: T&T Clark, 1968.

———. "Put k effektivnomu propovedovaniyu" ("The Way to Effective Preaching"). *Put Bogopoznaniia*. 7 (2001) 5–20.

Sharp, Douglas P., "Kto takiie baptisty segodnia? Razmishleniia o vosstanovlenii baptistskoi identichnosti i kharaktera: bogoslovskoie obrazovaniie kak akt protivostoianiia gospodstvuyuschei kulture" ("Who are Baptists today? Reflections on Rebuilding of Baptist Identity and Character: Theological Education as an Act of Resistance to Culture"). *Put Bogopoznaniia* 4 (1998) 102–21.

Shevzov, Vera. *Russian Orthodoxy on the Eve of Revolution*. Oxford: Oxford University Press, 2004.

Shutkin, Nicolay, "Selo Ivanovka" ("The Village of Ivanovka"). In *Zemlia Khokhol'skaia (The Land of Khokhol)*, edited by Nikolaii G. Pegarkov, 55–61. Voronezh, Russia: Volkhovitinogo, 1998.

Sinichkin, Alexey. "Istoriia zhurnala 'Baptist'" ("The History of the Journal *Baptist*"). http://www.rusbaptist.stunda.org/vsjo-radi-missii.htm.

———. "Vlast i sluzhiteli na etape formirovaniia VSEKHB" ("Authorities and Ministers at the Stage of Formation of AUCECB"). In *Traditsiia podgotovki sluzhitelei v bratstve evangelskikh khristian-baptistov. Istoriia i perspectivi: sbornik statei (Tradition of Preparation of Ministers in the Brotherhood of Evangelical Christians–Baptists: History and Prospects: Collection of Articles)*. Moscow: RUECB, 2013.

Sipko, Yuri K. "Zhit' po Biblii ili po "pon'iatiiam"?" ("To Live According to the Bible or According to 'Unwritten Laws?'"). http://ysipko.ru/zhit-po-biblii-ili-po-ponyatiyam.

Spurgeon, Charles Haddon. "Rabota presvitera i propovednika nad soboi" ("The work of the pastor and the preacher on himself"). *Bratskii Vestnik* 2 (1958).

Stassen, Glen H. "A New Vision." In *Authentic Transformation: A New Vision of Christ and Culture*, edited by Glen H. Stassen et al., 191–268. Nashville: Abingdon, 1996.

Tetereviatnikov, Konstantin. "Perspectivi vospitaniia sluzhitelei: proshloie, nastoiashcheie i budushcheie" ("The Prospects of Forming of Ministers: Past, Present, and Future").

Bibliography

In *Traditsiia podgotovki sluzhitelei v bratstve evangelskikh khristian-baptistov. Istoriia i perspectivi: sbornik statei (Tradition of Preparation of Ministers in the Brotherhood of Evangelical Christians-Baptists: History and Prospects: Collection of Articles)*. Moscow: RUECB, 2013.

Thunberg, Lars. *Man and the Cosmos: The Vision of Saint Maximus the Confessor.* Crestwood, NY: St. Vladimir's Seminary Press, 1985.

Timchenko, Irina. "Muzikalnaia osnova bogosluzheniia evangelskikh khristian-baptistov" ("Music Foundations the Worship of Evangelical Christians–Baptists"). *Put Bogopoznaniia* 1 (1996) 61–73.

Timoshenko, Mikhail. "Kafedra" ("The Pulpit"). *Baptist* 36 (1911) 285–86.

Tkachuk, Vitalii. *Metody i printsipy tolkovaniia sviashchennogo pisaniia (Methods and Principles of Interpretation of the Holy Scripture)*. Lutsk, Ukraine: Centr Khristianskoi Zhizni Ukraini, 2000.

Torbet, Robert G., et al. *A History of the Baptists*. Odessa: Bogomislie, 1996.

Tuck, Willian Powell. *Our Baptist Tradition*. Macon, GA: Smyth and Helwys, 1993.

Vandevelde, Pol. *The Task of the Interpreter: Text, Meaning, and Negotiation*. Pittsburgh: University of Pittsburgh Press, 2005.

Vanhoozer, Kevin J. "Four Theological Faces of Biblical Interpretation." In *Reading Scripture with the Church: Toward a Hermeneutic for Theological Interpretation*, edited by A. K. M. Adam et al., 131–42. Grand Rapids: Baker Academic, 2006.

Vernadsky, George. *A History of Russia*, 3rd ed. New Haven, CT: Yale University Press, 1951.

Vetelev, Alexander. *Istoriia propovednichestva russkoi pravoslavnoi tserkvi: Uchebnoie posobie dlia studentov 4-go klassa (The History of Preaching of Russian Orthodox Church: Study Guide for 4th Year Students)*. Sergiev Posad, Russia: Moskovskaia Dukhovnaia Seminariia, 2006.

Waldron, Peter. "Religious Toleration in Late Imperial Russia." In *Civil Rights in Imperial Russia*, edited by Olga Crisp and Linda Edmondson, 103–20. Oxford: Clarendon, 1989.

Wardin, Albert W., Jr. "How Indigenous was the Baptist Movement in the Russian Empire?" *Journal of European Baptist Studies* 9.2 (2009) 29–37.

———. "Penetration of Baptists into the Russian Empire in the Nineteenth Century." *Journal of European Baptist Studies* 7.3 (2007) 34–47.

Weber, Max. *The Theory of Social and Economic Organizations*. Glencoe, IL: Free Press, 1947.

Welch, Sharon D. *A Feminist Ethics of Risk*. Minneapolis: Fortress, 1990.

Wink, Walter. *Engaging the Powers: Discernment and Resistance in a World of Domination*. Minneapolis: Fortress, 1992.

———. *Naming the Power: The Language of Power in the New Testament*. Philadelphia: Fortress, 1984.

———. *The Powers that Be: Theology for a New Millennium*. New York: Doubleday, 1998.

Wright, Nigel G. *Free Church, Free State: The Positive Baptist Vision*. Carlisle, UK: Paternoster, 2005.

———. *New Baptists, New Agenda*. Carlisle, UK: Paternoster, 2002.

Yarigin, Nicolay N. *Evangelskoie dvizheniie v Volgo-Viatskom regione (Evangelical Movement in Volgo-Viatski Region)*. Moscow: Akademicheskii Proiekt, 2004.

Yoder, John Howard. *Body Politics: Five Practices of the Christian Community Before the Watching World*. Nashville: Herald, 1992.

Bibliography

———. "How H. Richard Nieburh Reasoned: A Critique of *Christ and Culture*." In *Authentic Transformation: A New Vision of Christ and Culture*, edited by Glen H. Stassen et al., 31–90. Nashville: Abingdon, 1996.

———. *The Politics of Jesus: Vicit Agnus Noster*, 2nd ed. Grand Rapids: Eerdmans, 1994.

Zacek, Judith Cohen, "The Russian Bible Society and the Russian Orthodox Church." *Church History* 35 (1966) 411–37.

Zemskov, Victor. "GULAG (Istoriko-sotsialnii aspekt)" ("GULAG [Historical-Sociological Aspect]"). *Sotsiologicheskiie Issledovaniia* 6 (1991) 10–27; 7 (1991) 3–16.

Zhidkov, Yakov I. "Poriadok propovedi na nashikh sluzheniiakh" ("The Order of Preaching in our Services"). *Bratskii Vestnik* 3–4 (1955) 58–60.

———. "Vzgliad Nazad" ("Retrospect"). *Bratskii Vestnik* 1 (1948) 5–10.

Zhuk, Sergei. *Russia's Lost Reformation: Peasants, Millennialism, and Radical Sects in Southern Russia and Ukraine, 1830–1917*. Washington D.C.: Woodrow Wilson Center, 2004.

www.ingramcontent.com/pod-product-compliance
Lightning Source LLC
Chambersburg PA
CBHW070922180426
43192CB00037B/1725